Paulo Freire
at the Institute

Edited by
**Maria de Figueiredo-Cowen
and Denise Gastaldo**

The 'Brazilia
INSTITUTE
University

D1427230

British Library Cataloguing in Publication Data.
A catalogue record for this book is available from the British Library.

ISBN 0 85473 429 5

© Institute of Education
University of London

January 1995

Typography and Design by Joan Rose
Reprographics Department
Institute of Education, University of London
20 Bedford Way, London WC1H 0AL

Printed by
Formara Limited
16 The Candlemakers, Temple Farm Industrial Estate
Southend on Sea, Essex SS2 6RX

Distributed by B&MBC Distribution Services
9 Headlands Business Park
Ringwood, Hants BH24 3PB
Tel: 0425 471160

Contents

Foreword

When Paulo Freire visited the Institute in October 1993, he turned a lecture to some 800 people into an intensely personal conversation. It was as if a few of us were drinking coffee together, and listening and talking seriously. That gift of immediacy with an audience is a rare one. It is a particular example of the Freirian idea of becoming what we want to become. In this case, one of this century's great educators sharing that greatness with us as great teacher.

Paulo Freire does not educate us by reflecting on our experience. He reflects on his own experience. The nature of that experience and the reading, writing and reflection which illuminate it, give him his peculiar power to illuminate our own experience as educators, and our own lives as people.

"Will no one rid me of this turbulent priest?" an English king once said of an Archbishop who opposed him. Paulo Freire was treated as a dangerous priest in an earlier part of his life and barely survived that experience. The paradox is that Paulo Freire, though capable of anger and irreverent wit as the anecdotes in his lecture show, is personally the least turbulent of men. His thought is coherent, his manner quiet, the articulation of his philosophy sophisticated and elegant. With humility and determination he follows his argument wherever it leads. He reflects on the sources of oppression and on the possibilities for men and women to take control of their lives. His messages are radical; but his power to influence comes through and out of the word – through new ways of thinking and feeling.

It is with pleasure that I invite the reader to investigate Paulo Freire's new ideas in the following lectures, essays and discussions presented at the Institute of Education, and to take from Paulo Freire whatever the reader's previous experience permits. And perhaps a little more.

Sir Peter Newsam
Director, Institute of Education
Autumn 1993

Introduction

Paulo Freire in London – twenty years on

For many years academics and graduate students at the Institute of Education had been hoping to have Paulo Freire here and to discuss his work with him. A number of attempts were made, unsuccessfully. Finally, on October 25 1993 at 9:30 Paulo Freire walked up the steps onto the Logan Hall stage. In the audience, there were around 800 people – academics, teachers, students, press representatives, and professionals from different areas – every one waiting to listen to Paulo. For some, that occasion was memorable for being the first opportunity to meet the Brazilian philosopher and pedagogue; for others, the occasion was even more exciting, because it meant a re-encounter after 20 years.

Paulo Freire did not arrive alone. For this special occasion, Dr Ana Maria de Araújo Freire had also been invited for her expertise on the history of literacy in Brazil. This expertise is unique: her scholastic work has interacted with that of her husband, Paulo. Ana Maria came to talk about Freire's contribution to literacy in Brazil.

Both Paulo and Nita, as he affectionately calls Ana Maria, were welcomed by Professor Peter Mortimore, Deputy Director of the Institute of Education, and by His Excellency Paulo Tarso Flecha de Lima, Brazilian Ambassador in London. Paulo Freire's talk was the first in a new joint initiative between the Institute of Education and the Brazilian Embassy, and Paulo Freire's Seminar inaugurated the 'Brazilian Educators' Lecture Series.

This first seminar of the Lecture Series was only possible thanks to the joint efforts of a number of people and institutions: the University of London Institute of Education, the Brazilian Ministry of External Relations, the Cultural Section of the Brazilian Embassy, and the Banco do Brasil S.A. – London Branch. The Seminar Advisers were: David Warren, Secretary and Academic Registrar, Institute of Education; Flávio de Lima Rocha, Cultural Attaché, Brazilian Embassy; Robert Cowen, Department of International and Comparative Education, Institute of Education; and Marcos Formiga, International Cooperation, CNPq, Brazil. It is also important to acknowledge the daily work over several months of our colleagues who were research students at the Institute of Education, and who helped us in the organization of the Seminar: Ana Helena Rubano, Ana Maria Lakomy and Denise Trento de Souza.

Finally, the special thanks of the Editors must go to: Phillip Drummond (English, Media and Drama) and Tom Waldron (Educational Media Services) who recorded the Seminar; Jill Roche, Joan Rose, and their colleagues in Reprographics; Cathy Bird, the Institute Conference Organizer; Marina Kern, Paulo and Ana Maria Freire's secretary, for providing information for the Appendix; Robert Cowen (DICE), for crucial advice in putting together this project; and, of course, the Discussants..

Maria de Figueiredo-Cowen
(Brazilian Lektor)

Denise Gastaldo
(Department of Policy Studies and
Department of International and Comparative Education)

Editorial

Paulo Freire is known worldwide as an educator. His theoretical work has illuminated projects of formal and non-formal education at different levels, from literacy programmes to higher education, in a variety of countries. His work is studied in universities and colleges of education throughout the world. **Pedagogy of the Oppressed**, for example, can be read in English, French, German, Japanese, Spanish, and many other languages. However, in the last five years Paulo Freire's work has not been easily available to readers other than Portuguese-speakers. For instance, **Pedagogy of Hope** was published in English only in 1994; *Professora Sim, Tia Não* (1993) – "Teacher Yes, Auntie No", *Política e Educação* (1993) – "Politics and Education", and *Cartas a Cristina* (1994) – "Letters to Cristina" have not been translated yet.

This volume is therefore thought of as an opportunity to make widely available Paulo Freire's talks, which are based around issues he has discussed in recent publications in Portuguese. This book is shaped by dialogue: Paulo Freire answers specific questions raised by his discussants and the Seminar audience. Most of all, this publication is an opportunity to 'listen' to Freire's reflections on his own educational practice. It is also a first hand narrative on some of the themes Freire has been exploring throughout his life.

This book is built around a central topic: the educational theory of Paulo Freire. Freire himself is of course the centre of the volume. His talks and discussions are presented here in three chapters. Chapter 2 is the talk of Paulo Freire on progressive education. Freire chose to start the Seminar discussing the virtues of the progressive teacher. He explores the impossibility of neutral practice in education, and the virtues that should shape the practice of the progressive teacher: humility, tolerance, love, and coherence, among others. Chapter 5 contains Freire's comments on topics developed by the discussants. In Chapter 6, Freire discusses the issues of neutrality, respect for the students, epistemological curiosity, and international financial aid, whilst answering questions raised by the audience.

In order to introduce some specific features of Paulo Freire's life and work in education, the Editors discuss, in Chapter 1, Freire's professional and personal experiences and their impact on the development of his theoretical work. The Editors also analyse the concept of 'progressive education'. Ideas about political practice, oppression, competence, utopias, and education as political practice are the basis for this analysis.

In Chapter 3 Ana Maria de Araújo Freire presents the contribution of Paulo Freire to literacy in Brazil. She describes many initiatives in which Freire has been involved to promote literacy from his first works with adult non-formal education to his experience as Secretary of Education of the City of São Paulo. Ana Maria Freire analyses Freire's political-pedagogy and literacy 'method' in the context of Brazilian history.

Chapter 4 contains the presentations of the three discussants invited to comment on particular issues arising in or from Freire's work. The first discussant, Gunther Kress, concentrates on semiosis, literacy and transformation. Taking examples from European newspapers, he raises questions about the construction of meaning, whilst analysing education in a multicultural society. The second discussant, Jennifer Chew, talks about literacy among sixth form students. From her teaching experience in England and South Africa she questions whether or not a political project has meaning without formal (linguistic) knowledge. Roy Carr-Hill, the third discussant, is concerned with mass literacy campaigns. Using examples of how Freire's political conception of education can be misused in simple political party propaganda, he raises the question of whether a mass literacy campaign in Brazil in the 1960s would have really worked, as Freire suggests.

It is hoped that this book will contribute to the understanding of Freire's work in two different ways: firstly, distinct moments of Freire's professional and personal life are discussed to illuminate how his theoretical work was construed; secondly, through Freire's own narrative, a sense of closeness is created between the reader and Freire's educational practice. As a writer, Paulo Freire presents through his books the scope of his interests. As a speaker, he shows himself as the progressive educator. His clarity and consistency, his sense of indignation and of humility can perhaps act as a source of inspiration to the challenge of being, or becoming, a progressive teacher.

Maria de Figueiredo-Cowen
Denise Gastaldo

Paulo Freire in the Nineties: Life Experience and Progressive Education

Denise Gastaldo
Maria de Figueiredo-Cowen

> *"No one is born fully formed: it is through self-experience in the world that we become what we are".*
>
> Paulo Freire[1]

INTRODUCTION

A striking feature of Paulo Freire's work is its contextualisation of education in historical, cultural, political, and social perspective. It is our aim in this essay to contextualise Paulo Freire in his own historical, cultural, political and social environment in order to promote a better understanding of his thought. How did Paulo Freire become Paulo Freire? In which context did he live and work? Which circumstances led him to become a radical thinker? Is Paulo Freire now different from the Paulo Freire of the cultural circles[2] in the fifties and sixties? Or from the Paulo Freire in exile in the seventies? Or from the Paulo Freire back to Brazil, after the Amnesty, in the eighties? With these questions in mind, we will attempt to contextualise Paulo Freire and to explore his concept of progressive[3] education.

This essay is divided into two sections. The first one will attempt to relate the trajectory of Freire's life to his educational work. This relationship will be examined in three periods: (a) from Freire's childhood to the creation of his literacy method; (b) Freire's life and work in exile; and (c) Freire's work in Brazil in the eighties and nineties. The second section will be devoted to the Freirian concept of progressive education, a concept vital to the understanding of Freire's work. Five aspects will be discussed: (a) education as a political practice; (b) the difficulties of progressive education; (c) education as a tool for unveiling oppression; (d) education and competence; and (e) education and utopias.

The purpose of this essay is thus to provide the reader with some insights into Freire's life experience and the building up of his theory. The essay also contributes to making available to English speakers the most recent ideas of Freire on education as these have been formulated in his latest publications in Portuguese.

1. PAULO FREIRE LEARNS FROM EXPERIENCE

1.1. From Childhood to a Literacy Method

The social commitment that is so clear in Paulo Freire's work comes from many experiences. Perhaps the first dramatic experience he went through, with considerable effect on his thought, was the financial difficulty faced by his family when he was a child[4]. Freire's parents were forced to leave an urban environment and went to a more rural area. Since then he has been in direct contact with the world of the poor. Looking back into his childhood Freire acknowledges a change in what he calls his personal sociology and psychology:

> *My family, from the middle classes, had to leave our house in Recife to live in Jaboatão. There was that magical idea that things could get better only through moving from Recife. However, things got worse. This brought about a fundamental change in my life. My universe expanded.*[5]

Within this expanded universe, Freire came in direct contact with many forms of prejudice and discrimination. He noted the oppressive conditions under which women, and particularly black women, were treated in society. However he acknowledges that the two kinds of prejudice that had a major impact on him in his twenties were class and racial oppression[6].

No single experience is able to create the foundation of such a powerful theory as Paulo Freire's. Fundamental to the building up of his theory was the time Paulo Freire spent in the *SESI – Serviço Social da Indústria* (1946-56)[7]. As a teacher and a director of the SESI Education and Cultural Division he had close contact with students and their parents who belonged to the lower levels of the social strata. Once again Freire experienced the struggles of the underprivileged[8]. It was at that time that he started to conceptualise education from a political perspective. In his own opinion[9] the time he worked at SESI was vital to the formulation of the **Pedagogy of the Oppressed**. Freire explains the complexities of how he became himself:

Interestingly enough, the context of my childhood and adolescence, the familiarity with both the evil of the powerful groups, and the fragility – which needs to become strength – of the powerless people, and with the essential time spent in SESI, full of "welding" and "bindings" of old and pure "guessings", these elements together made my new knowledge, which emerged in a critical way, full of meaning. I "read" the raison d'être (or part of it) of the tangles of books – the ones I had not read, and those still to be written – that would later illuminate my living memory. Marx, Lukács, Fromm, Gramsci, Fanon, Memmi, Sartre, Kosik, Agnes Heller, M. Ponty, Simone Weill, Arendt, Marcuse . . . [10]

Freire gained a national reputation in the early sixties with his 'method' for teaching illiterate adults. This method was a result of theoretical thinking and writing about his previous experience as a teacher of Portuguese, as a researcher and teacher at SESI, in the Movement of Popular Culture, and at the Department of Cultural Community Services (*Serviço de Extensão Cultural*) at the University of Recife[11].

From a local experiment in Angicos, a town in the Brazilian State of Pernambuco, the method reached the whole country. The results from the Angicos experience were so impressive that President João Goulart, having visited it, decided to implement the model nationally. Paulo Freire was invited in June 1963 to co-ordinate this 'National Programme of Literacy'. The programme was officially launched in January 1964.

Freire's literacy method was a revolutionary proposal in a country where illiteracy was a chronic social disease. Teachers became excited by the educational breakthrough which the method represented. It was aimed at the masses of the working class and rural population that had been historically excluded from any kind of educational assistance. Soon a variety of different training courses on the method spread all over the country. Many teachers understood the possible impact that such a method could have in the search for the social justice which the country badly needed.

However, the different kinds of transformation that the campaigns might have caused will never be known. The plan was to teach five million Brazilians how to read and write in two years, but the change in the political system with the coup d' état on April 1st 1964 destroyed an incipient experience for ideological reasons[12]. The 'Paulo Freire Method' was considered subversive. The National Programme was closed down, and those who designed the Programme were persecuted. According to the military government, Freire was a communist and subversive. Freire himself explains that he was not a member of the Communist Party, but he was subversive. His pedagogy aimed at subverting the traditional power relations in the educational setting and in society. He was suggesting a democratic experience based on the needs and dreams of the underprivileged classes[13].

1.2. Paulo Freire's theory and practice abroad

In Brazil Paulo Freire was blocked from implementing in full what he wanted to do in adult education. He went to jail, and later into exile (1964). Freire's experience in exile was a dual one: he was an academic in universities of worldwide reputation, in Germany, in the USA, and in Switzerland; and he extended his political and pedagogical ideas in helping revolutionary and popular movements in Africa, Europe, and Latin America[14].

Looking back on those years of exile, Freire mentions how gratifying that dual experience was. As an academic, he tried to implement fully his political and pedagogical practice. He was not completely successful though: not because he faced any kind of political constraints, but because the nature of the educational process imposed its own limits. Nevertheless, he was not unhappy, having learnt a great deal from this unfulfilled objective[15]. He also felt gratified in his political and pedagogical activism, as he points out:

> *This was a great satisfaction – as a thinker about educational practice, I was understood and invited by active militants to a dialogue about their own (armed or unarmed) struggle. This satisfaction accompanied me during the seventies and has lasted until today . . . In addition to the satisfaction of those encounters, there was the joy of many others, in every corner of the world, where I met progressive people who used to dream the possible dream of changing the world.[16]*

The sixteen years which Freire spent in exile were very productive: he published, he taught, and he supported political progressive groups. Freire never resented the reasons that forced him to leave Brazil. He understood his exile as a necessity for the Right which had as its major aim to prevent intellectuals like Paulo Freire from working with the masses and promoting literacy and critical consciousness. However, exile had an ambivalent undertone for him. He manifested during these years traits of cultural resistance, for example, a non-conscious unwillingness to learn other languages, and a non-conscious (at that time) rejection of any other cuisine. He tried to eat only Brazilian food. In his own interpretation, this cultural resistance had to do with the fear of harming his Brazilian identity[17]. This cultural resistance was so strongly felt that even today, after over fourteen years of re-encounter with Brazil, he looks anxiously for Brazilian cuisine when he travels abroad.

While in exile, Paulo Freire became a founder member of the Workers Party (*Partido dos Trabalhadores*) in Brazil. Professor Moacir Gadotti represented him at the foundation of the party. It was Freire's first political affiliation. He argued that it was the first political party in Brazilian history that originated at grass roots level. This party resulted directly from the need that unions and workers had to organise themselves. Only later did the intellectuals of the Left join in[18].

1.3. Paulo Freire back in Brazil

On his return from exile, Freire used to say that he realized how fully Brazilian he still was, having kept even his Northeastern accent. From his point of view, the exile had been both a rupture and a difficult learning process on how to live – culturally, politically, and emotionally – in a 'borrowed' context in which he was removed from his own reality[19].

The return also provided Paulo Freire with a multiplicity of new experiences. The first new experience was political. In the 1982 political campaigns in São Paulo State, he held many small scale meetings with workers. He once again perceived the oppression of the dominant class inside the minds of the oppressed. As an example, Freire tells the story of a worker who said he would not vote for Lula (the candidate of the Workers Party for Governor of São Paulo). He explained his reasons: Lula is, like him, a worker; Lula does not have the expected command of Portuguese to be state governor because he had not attended school long enough. The worker went on, saying: "Could you imagine what would happen if the Queen of England visits Brazil again? Lula's wife, as First Lady, does not have the necessary skills to host a Queen"[20].

Freire also re-experienced Brazil through university teaching and seminars around the country. He taught and talked to people who had never met him before, but who had secretly read copies of his books, and who had fought the dictatorship which had sent Paulo Freire into exile.

This fresh experience of Brazil led to a new creativity for Paulo Freire. He has been writing vigorously especially in the nineties. He has been re-exploring Vygotsky and Piaget, theoreticians considered by Freire to be essential in studies of literacy. Freire points out that in his early writing career, Vygotsky was unknown in Brazil, Piaget's work was scarcely known, and Emilia Ferreiro was just an adolescent. Freire realised how influential Piaget, Vygotsky, and Ferreiro have been in the development of the 'constructivist movement' in Brazil in the late 1980s and in the 1990s. Freire acknowledges that today child literacy programmes are much better in Brazil. He also emphasizes the role that his work plays and has played in this improvement:

> *I do not want to lack modesty, but I have to say that it is not possible to talk about constructivism without mentioning Paulo Freire. The foundations of constructivism are embedded in my work. In this sense, my contribution is very much alive in Brazil today. . . . the combination of my theory and practices with Emilia Ferreiro's research improves both Paulo's and Emilia's work. I find it a pity that Emilia does not use a political approach.*[21]

Another aspect of Freire's intellectual work has been a renewed commitment to the progressive movement in education. He is constantly advancing his theories on education as a means towards freedom. He has not permitted himself to be affected by the 'new' Democratic Right which coopted his method in the eighties in Brazil. From his point of view[22], the Right coopted Freire as it had Marx, for example. This is what is to be expected from the Right. It is also expected that the Right will try to break a progressive instrument – like his method – which tries to promote social change through class struggle. Freire sees this position of cooptation as a feature of the Right. He thinks that what the Left has to do is to establish and develop its own ethics, rejecting the traditional procedures of the Right.

Within the ideological frame of the progressive movement, Paulo Freire had the opportunity to implement new educational policies in the municipal schools of São Paulo, during his term of office as Secretary of Education (1989-1991). He was reluctant to accept the position which would become his first political appointment. However, he never ceased to be an educator *per se*. As a progressive educator his challenge was to implement new policies along the lines of his pedagogical project in over 662 schools, with 710,000 students, and 39,614 staff in a municipality with a population of 11.4 million inhabitants. Among numerous achievements, Freire was able to increase the student retention rate from 79.46% to 87.7% in primary schools. Very important was the implementation of the MOVA-São Paulo (Literacy Training Movement) programme, based on a partnership between social movements and the Secretariat of Education[23].

Paulo Freire enters the nineties with a stronger worldwide reputation for his work in education. In 1994 he already had twenty six doctorates *honoris causa* and many international awards[24].

This paper has tried so far to outline the impact of Freire's life on his work as a pedagogue, an academic, and an administrator of education. It is time now to discuss the concept of progressive education embedded in Freire's latest publications.

2. THE FREIRIAN CONCEPT OF PROGRESSIVE EDUCATION

2.1. Education as a Political Practice

Freire's lifetime experiences have led him to a very political understanding of education. His assumption that education is a political act denies the possibility that education can be neutral. For Freire, to teach how to read words is only meaningful if it also involves teaching about how to read the world.

There is a huge emphasis in Freire's work on the political dimension of education in the classroom. He argues that teachers ought to act politically outside and inside schools. Teachers act politically in activities such as strikes or the boycotting of policies; but when in contact with children or adults within the classroom they sometimes 'pretend' to be non-political persons. Freire stresses that "the interior of the school is also my exterior"[25]. By that he means that the space where the teacher and children interact is first of all a political one. Consequently, to be an educator means to be political.

Teachers are constantly facing political options: in the selection of curriculum contents, and in the ways they use authority, for example. It is true that there is no complete coherence in social practices. Nevertheless, political trends can be identified in the way teachers carry out their work. This is what has permitted Freire to distinguish between the conservative and the progressive teacher[26].

The progressive teacher rejects two common approaches to education. First s/he rejects the naive idea that education is the driving force to transform society. Second s/he also rejects the notion that education has no transformative power which means rejecting the idea that educators must wait for society to reach some level of transformation for some form of progessive teaching to be introduced[27]. The progressive teacher is aware of the limitations of educational practice. But s/he must act within the possibilities which the educational process offers so that s/he will be able to promote critical consciousness, and practices of transformation.

Progressive education includes some specific features. It unveils oppressions which are taken for granted in society. It also means a strong commitment to dreams and utopias which must be made explicit. Above all it is an everyday task, but it is also a difficult one.

2.2. The difficulties of progressive education

The progressive teacher is undoubtedly faced with many challenges. It is a lifetime practice. S/he has to try to overcome the intrinsic difficulties of the process. Success in overcoming the challenges depends greatly upon the ability to learn from both theory and experience.

According to Freire[28], one of the difficulties in being progressive is the inconsistency between discourse and practice. The progressive discourse becomes meaningless when accompanied by authoritarian practice. Conversely, authoritarian practice becomes discourse. This is the case, for example, in what is happening in some state schools in Brazil in major urban centres. Teachers and pupils have different cultural and social backgrounds. Challenges come out of these differences but are not overcome by teachers. Looking for a 'simple' and/or traditional solution, rather than engaging themselves in a democratic dialogue with pupils, teachers choose to act in an authoritarian way. They thus impose their own values as the proper codes of behaviour and attitude in the classroom.

However, the reverse, i.e. the belief that to be progressive is to adopt a laissez-faire policy in the classroom, is not the solution. This would be a denial of the teacher's role as organizer or as challenger of the educational process. Progressive education can only be guaranteed with the democratic intervention of the educator[29]. Again the best tool for progressive teachers is the practice of dialogue in the classroom. Dialogue is a mediator of power. It gives to each individual in the classroom the opportunity to express her/his own views, to question and even challenge the power which emanates from knowledge.

Therefore, to be progressive means above all to act democratically. It should be noted however that sometimes this progressive practice is mistakenly reduced to a political-party position or to propaganda. This simplistic educational practice must be avoided. Politics goes far beyond party campaigns. The progressive teacher must always be aware of the real meaning of politics in educational practice.

Another challenge faced by the progressive teacher is how to maintain a steady level of criticism. This practice should be a constant one. To have moments of criticism rather than criticism as a practice is to narrow down progressive action. It is in the experience of each day that students learn and confront learning with theory. It is in this context that progressive practice happens through: (i) the critical analysis of events; (ii) the challenge of minds about the 'easy' explanations of social relations; and, (iii) the questioning of the historical truth. Questioning is at the very centre of progressive practice.

2.3. Unveiling Oppression through Questioning

An important element in Freire's concept of progressive praxis is the commitment teachers must have to the constant exercise of questioning. Unfortunately, many educators associate knowledge with irrefutable certainties. Perhaps the intention is to help students to learn the truth. Furthermore, the method most teachers traditionally use is to underpin their assumptions with historical and scientific facts, unaware that knowledge is social, active and critically produced.

The educational practice that excludes different interpretations of the same reality, or denies any approaches based on doubt and criticisms, forces upon the students the truth of the dominant groups in society. Such an approach only reinforces the power of the teacher, produces a mythification of knowledge, and encourages non-critical analysis among students[30].

Conversely, to challenge the 'truths' is the progressive approach which Freire suggests. This challenge implies, as Freire points out, that political clarity and scientific competence are necessary for the developement of a progressive practice:

> There is another task to be fulfilled at the school in spite of hegemonic power – that of making clear a reality darkened by the dominant ideology. Obviously, this is the task progressive teachers have: not only to teach with competence curriculum contents, but also to unveil the world of oppression through their teaching.[31]

Reality is socially constructed. The dominant class has a variety of ways to exert power. One of them is to create oppressive patterns within social relationships. Being so deeply spread, these patterns are even embodied within the minds of the oppressed. Freire points out that the oppressor lives in and rules the body of the oppressed[32]. Such oppression has been so constantly reinforced through time, that it has been taken for granted as a normal part of daily life. Progressive practice has the major task of being always guided by the principle of unveiling reality and of reaching a critical consciousness. Reasoning beyond appearances helps to identify oppression in both internal and external worlds.

Unveiling oppression through challenging 'the' truth is also part of Freire's concept of education as a political practice. However, in order to encourage critical analysis and demystify knowledge, competence is required from the progressive teacher.

2.4. To be Progressive is to be Competent

The progressive teacher has to cultivate a number of virtues in order to become more competent[33]. These virtues are: humility, affection, tolerance, decisiveness, confidence, impatient patience, verbal parsimony, and joy of life. These virtues are intimately related to Freire's concept of education. He conceptualizes education as an activity which is both emotional and cognitive. Critical judgement alone does not make education. Education is an experience of the whole body[34].

In addition to virtues, the progressive teacher must have a strong sense of professionalism, especially in 'third world' countries where there are so many lay teachers, used as educational manpower, earning low wages and reproducing an image of non-professionalism in education[35]. Freire points out that to be professional is to be technically and emotionally prepared for the educational task:

> The task of teaching is a professional task. However, it requires affection, creativity, and scientific competence; but, it rejects scientific narrowness. It also requires a capacity to fight for freedom, without which the teaching task fades away.[36]

Another element in competent educational practice is the respect for the learning process which the individual student experiences. Students understand they have the capacity to learn. They grasp the meanings which emerge from information, and discover that they themselves are active participants in this process through creating new knowledge and criticizing formulated knowledge. The competent progressive teacher promotes such processes by taking into account the previous skills of the students, even the most basic ones. Teachers should be aware of the differences among students, and especially of the differences they already have in their 'reading of the world':

> *The student needs to have full responsibility as an actor with*
> *knowledge and not as a recipient of the teacher's discourse. In a*
> *final analysis this is the major political act of teaching. Among*
> *other elements this is the one which makes the progressive educator*
> *different from the reactionary educator.*[37]

Within the frame of education as a political act, the progressive teacher combines scientific expertise, and pedagogical and personal skills. In the personal profile of the teacher Freire emphasizes the idea of utopias. For Freire, dreams are inherent to all human beings. Progressive teachers above all must make these dreams explicit. This is an ethical duty.

2.5. Progressive Education and Utopias

The progressive teacher ought to be committed to dreams which should not be kept to her/himself but disclosed to the students. It should be noted that in presenting his/her utopia the teacher must make it clear that the utopia is her/his. Otherwise it is unethical. Further, students must be told that there are dreams other than the teacher's.

According to Paulo Freire to dream is to be able to perceive different possible routes to make the dream real. It is also to react against the abuses of power that make the life of so many so difficult. Of course there will always be obstacles to dreams, but being conscious of these obstacles without envisaging possible routes is a hopeless process because it does not help to overcome constraints. The possibility for transformation dwells precisely in changing what is possible to change today with the aim at achieving in the future what seems impossible today.

Having utopias implies the denial of a mechanistic explanation of History. This means, according to Freire, that the progressive teacher has to understand her/himself as a subject of History, rather than a mere object. S/he must adopt an attitude which is critically optimistic, refusing both a naive optimism and a fatalist pessimism[38]. Freire points out:

> *One of the tasks of the progressive educator is, through a serious*
> *and proper political analysis, to unveil the possibilities for hope,*
> *no matter what the obstacles are. Without hope, little can be done*
> *because we rarely struggle; when we do struggle whether hopelessly*
> *or desperately, our fight is a suicidal act; it is a face to face struggle*
> *out of revenge.*[39]

Behind the notion of utopia in Freire's work is his category of analysis "untested feasibility". Utopia plays an important role in leading to every-day struggle against oppression. Both oppressive and liberating forces are inside each individual. Freire stresses that although the conditioners of oppression are many and strong, there is the possibility of overcoming oppression within personal and social life. "Untested feasibility" is an element of belief and creativity that can be present in both individual and collective dreams. The belief is that there are feasible actions available in the current moment that may produce change. The challenge is that they are untested. Ana Maria Freire[40] points out that to transform "untested feasibility" into reality, a praxis for liberation is essential, and those who share the same utopia have to reflect and identify the constraints on their utopia and together tackle specific situations that limit their fulfilment as human beings.

The relationship between student and teacher should be established through the mutual challenge of their utopias. It is through the process of education that they have the opportunity to construct and re-construct dreams aiming at, as progressive people, a more egalitarian and happier society.

CONCLUSION

Freire's contribution to the understanding of education goes far beyond education itself. It becomes a contribution to epistemology, philosophy and politics, among other forms of understanding and ways of acting. Freire has always denied any possible understanding of education as a neutral science. Theorizing upon his experiences and learning from them, Freire has been claiming a political status for education. It is this political status that has permitted him to discuss so clearly and directly the issues of oppression, liberation and empowerment.

Freire has been haunted by oppression, throughout his life: he has experienced oppression and has worked with oppressed people. The constant theme of oppression in Freire's work has helped him to illuminate his concern with the role education takes in liberating people. This is true for the **Pedagogy of the Oppressed** (1970), *Pedagogia da Esperança* – "Pedagogy of Hope" (1992), and *Professora Sim, Tia Não* – "Teacher Yes, Auntie No" (1993).

Oppression and liberation are the two poles between which the educational process takes place. The transformation from oppressed to liberated people can be achieved through education. Within Freire's theory of education students are empowered by being placed as subjects of the educational process. He also empowers teachers, acknowledging them as professionals who need high qualifications and who have power to promote critical consciousness. Thus, the science of education has been empowered with its inherent political strength towards transformation.

Although Freire has been writing for three decades on all these issues, his work has been perceived with different intensity, in different periods, and in different countries. Some educators privilege a particular theory that is 'fashionable' in a given moment. To those who naively and incorrectly say "Paulo Freire is outdated", he replies:

> *Outdated no. I am! Whoever wants to work in the area of popular education in Brazil or in Latin America, no matter which approach is chosen, has to read Paulo Freire. It can be a reading of agreement or disagreement, or both, even going beyond Paulo Freire. The only impossible reading is to deny my work.*[41]

It can be said that Freire has made a permanent contribution to studies of adult education, literacy, and popular education worldwide. In all these areas Freire stresses the relevance (and the limitations) of education as a social and political process. It is between the boundaries of the possibilities for transformation and the limitations implicit in any educational process that educators can develop a progressive practice unveiling oppression in a permanent critical reading of the world. The proposal of an educational-political process towards liberation and transformation of society is Freire's greatest contribution to education.

NOTES

1   Translated by the Editors from the original in Portuguese: *Ninguém nasce feito: é experimentando-nos no mundo que nós nos fazemos.* Freire, P. *Política e educação [Politics and education].* São Paulo: Cortez, 1993, p.79. Coleção Questões da Nossa Época, Vol.23.

2.   The cultural circles *(círculos de cultura)* were implemented by Paulo Freire in Brazil and later in Chile in the fifties and sixties. They aimed at promoting adult education through an original approach: teacher and learners jointly discussed and analysed issues in order to promote a better understanding of the meaning of culture. Adults become more aware of themselves as participants and creators of culture through their own work, popular art, cuisine, oral literature, and later, through their reading and writing.

3.   'Progressive', rather than 'progressist', is the English word chosen to translate 'progressista' from the Portuguese. Raymond Williams (*Keywords.* Glasgow: Collins Pub., 1983, pp.243-245) points out that in the mid 19th century English, 'progressist' was used as an opposite for 'conservative'. Progressive is the word selected here. In Freire's context, to be progressive means to promote changes based on a Leftist approach. Although progressive can be related to 'progress', this link cannot be applied to Freire's concept. The scientific discoveries and wealth accumulation have not necessarily promoted equality and social justice.

4.   Ana Maria Freire mentions the effects of the North American Great Depression on the economic life of Brazil in Chapter 3.

5.   Translated by the Editors: "Entrevista: Paulo Freire" [Interview: Paulo Freire]. *Teoria & Debate,* Jan-Mar 1992, p.32.

6.   Freire, P. and Macedo, D. "A dialogue with Paulo Freire", **in** McLaren, P. and Leonard, P. (eds) **Paulo Freire – a critical encounter.** London: Routledge, 1993, pp.170-171.

7.   SESI – Social Service for Industry – is an institution maintained by the National Confederation of Industry with the objective of promoting social assistance, and better living (education, health and housing) conditions for the workers in Brazilian industries.

8.   For further information see: Freire, P. *Pedagogia da esperança* [Pedagogy of hope]. São Paulo: Paz e Terra, 1993. pp.15-28.

9.   Freire, P. *Pedagogia da esperança,* op.cit., p.18.

10.   Translated by the Editors: Freire, P. *Pedagogia da esperança,* op.cit., p.19-20.

11.   See Freire, P. *Política e educação,* op.cit., p.79-88.

12.   See Chapters 4 (Roy Carr-Hill) and 5 for details.

13.   Entrevista: Paulo Freire. *Teoria & Debate,* op.cit. p.36.

14.   Examples of this militancy are found in *Pedagogia da esperança,* op.cit..

15.   Freire comments on some of these experiences in Chapter 6: Section 2, "On how to respect the context of the students and to be efficient".

16. Translated by the Editors: Freire, P. *Pedagogia da esperança,* op.cit., p.149.

17. Interview with the Editors, in London, 31 October 1993.

18. Entrevista: Paulo Freire. *Teoria & Debate,* op.cit., p.38.

19. Entrevista: Paulo Freire. *Teoria & Debate,* op.cit., p.39.

20. Freire, P. *Pedagogia da esperança,* op.cit., p.57.

21. Interview with the Editors, in London, 31 October 1993.

22. Interview with the Editors, in London, 31 October 1993.

23. For further information see: Torres, C., "Paulo Freire as Secretary of Education in the Municipality of São Paulo", *Comparative Education Review,* vol.38, no.2, pp.181-214, 1994.

24. See Appendix.

25. Interview with the Editors, in London, 31 October 1993.

26. See Chapter 2.

27. Freire, P. *Política e educação,* op.cit., p.54.

28. Freire, P. *Política e educação,* op.cit., p.54-58.

29. Freire, P. *Política e educação,* op.cit., p.52.

30. Approaches such as those are found at all levels of education. Recent research carried out at the University of Campinas among students in Teacher Education revealed strong criticisms regarding non-democratic lecturers who present themselves as the only holders of knowledge. See: Fini, L. "Repensando a psicologia educacional nos cursos de licenciatura" [Rethinking educational psychology courses in Teacher Education], *Educação* – PUCRS. Porto Alegre, Ano XVI, n. 25, 1993, pp.181-199.

31 Translated by the Editors: Freire, P. *Política e educação,* op.cit., p.53.

32. Freire, P. *Pedagogia da esperança,* op.cit., p.57.

33. For further information see: Chapter 2. See also *Professora sim, tia não [Teacher yes, auntie no]*. São Paulo: Olho D'água, 1993. Letter no. Four.

34. Freire, P. *Professora sim, tia não,* op cit., p.10.

35. The kindergartens are more susceptible to this kind of exploitation. See Chapter 6: Section 4, "International Financial Aid".

36. Translated by the Editors: Freire, P. *Professora sim, tia não,* op.cit., p.10.

37. Freire, P. *Pedagogia da esperança,* op.cit., pp.47-48.

38. Freire, P. *Política e educação,* op.cit., p.100.

39. Translated by the Editors: Freire, P. *Pedagogia da esperança,* op.cit., p.11.

40. Freire, Ana Maria A. Notes. In: Freire, P. *Pedagogia da esperança,* op.cit., pp.206-7.

41. Interview with the Editors, in London, 31 October 1993.

The Progressive Teacher

Paulo Freire

It is a great pleasure for me to be here at the Institute. I have been here before, twenty years ago. Today, although I am not feeling very well, I think I can survive at least one morning.

When I was flying from São Paulo to London, I asked myself about what could I talk about this morning. It is not always easy to speak about oneself. Sometimes I have asked myself: "What difficulty could there be in speaking about myself?" But it is difficult exactly because I do not know very well what should be the best approach. In the plane I remembered that I was bringing in my luggage three of my latest books, in Portuguese, to give to the Library of the Institute. The first one is **Pedagogy of Hope – a reencounter with the Pedagogy of the Oppressed**. This book emerged as a distortion of my initial intention – I had thought of writing a new introduction to the **Pedagogy of the Oppressed** in which I would say something about its history. I was attempting to write something about what the **Pedagogy of the Oppressed** did, and is still doing, through the languages into which it has been translated. But at some point in my writing, I discovered that what I was writing was not a new introduction. It was a new book. Then **Pedagogy of Hope** emerged. Instead of presenting the history of the **Pedagogy of the Oppressed**, I wrote something else – another book. This book is now being translated into English or "American".

My other book, on which my talk will be based this morning, is *Professora sim, Tia não*. Twenty years ago, a new dominant ideology became fashionable in Brazil. This new ideology attempted to de-professionalise the teacher, by suggesting that children call their teachers "aunties". The implicit message from the dominant groups was (and has been): 'How can you go on strike if you are aunties and the children are your nephews and nieces?' When I wrote this book I aimed at criticizing the de-professionalisation of the teacher. So, when I was asking myself what I could say here, I remembered the book *Professora sim, Tia não*, which is made up of 'Letters to teachers'. In one of these Letters I discuss the qualities or the virtues I think we should have as teachers if we are progressive teachers. I did not write about the virtues of the reactionary teacher because this is the duty of a reactionary thinker, which I am not. In that particular Letter what I did was to try to clarify what we have to do and what we should become (or try to become) by teaching in a progressive way.

My first point about this issue is: Why do I admit the existence of progressive teachers and the existence of reactionary teachers? If I understand education as a practice which cannot be neutral, I have to accept the dichotomy, progressive teachers and reactionary teachers, precisely because I do not accept the notion that all teachers are making something that is equal for all of us. I remember in the seventies the discussions I had in this country and also in Germany when I said that there is no neutrality in education. For some people that was a scandalous statement. Today I think I would not cause scandals when I say such things. Of course one of the elements of the educational practice whose technical name is "directivity" (*diretividade*) tells us something about the impossibility of being neutral in the practice of education. The "directivity" of education means that education starts from a given level and goes beyond itself. It also means that education has always implied utopias, dreams, desires, and values. I cannot simply say: I educate for nothing. Even the most naive educators and incompetent educators have to think about their own practice, and to think about why they work as a teacher. When, for example, we think about teachers' salaries in Brazil we realise that is rather difficult to remain in the profession. Today two hundred thousand teachers in São Paulo have been on strike for sixty-five days precisely because they insist on going on being teachers. This means that they have a kind of a dream. I am not a teacher because I was told that teaching is beautiful. I am a teacher because I love the beauty of teaching. There is a certain beauty in the very process of being a teacher. The bad aspect of this process is when, in our teaching, we contradict our dreams.

Thus the notion of "directivity" of education does not allow education to be a neutral process. We ought to clarify for ourselves what are our dreams, and how to put them into action. For example, I can have the dream – for me very ugly – of maintaining the *status quo* of society as it is now. It is a right which we have, the right of loving the stability of society. As with any other Brazilian, it would be perfectly possible for me to say, 'I am happy with the social situation of my country; with the number of people who cannot eat every day'. I then would work through a kind of educational practice in which I would try to maintain this situation with no attempt to unveil the reality. What is impossible, is to be neutral.

Sometimes we are not clear about what we would like to do in the world. One of our tasks, I think, is to clarify what we would like to do. It is during the process of acting as a teacher that we begin to understand what we would like to do. In my case, I am in the world because I would like to accomplish one of my tasks which is to contribute to changing the world. I discovered that very early in my childhood. I could not have come to the world in order to preserve the world as it is. I do not believe in immobility in history. I want to make some contribution to change, to transformation because it is by transforming the world that we can make it better.

When our task begins to become clear, we have to take charge of our praxis in a much clearer way. Then we discover the need to become more and more competent in order to do what we would like to do, to make what we would like to make. Along these lines, there is a Letter in which I discuss the qualities or the virtues of the progressive teacher. It is important to say that when I speak about qualities or virtues, I am not speaking about qualities we are born with. I am speaking about something which we make, we build by doing, by acting. I am sure that no one was born as she or he is; one becomes. We never **are**, because in order to be, it is necessary not to be. In other words, it is necessary to become. It is in becoming that I make myself. I am not, if I do not become. First I become. And I become to the extent to which I do what I would like to become. I have never received the gift of being a teacher, as I am. I became. Thus virtue means that I have to create quality by putting into practice the quality I would like to have.

One of the virtues of the progressive teacher is humility. To be humble does not mean to be afraid of doing things. On the contrary. To be humble pushes me towards acting without thinking that by acting I am the best. To be humble does not mean to love being loved. To be humble implies understanding oneself in the process of being with all the abilities and all the faults; to accept oneself as one who is becoming. To be humble is neither to deny nor to emphasize the values we think we have. It is to live more or less in peace. To be humble is not to be afraid to be criticized, not to be full of yourself because some people said you are interesting. To be humble means to resist compliments. In some cases compliments may be destructive. Sometimes it is necessary to be strong in order not to be destroyed by compliments.

We are not born with virtues or faults. We create them. Sometimes we do not have enough time in the world in order to learn these simple things. We are so interested in finding ourselves beautiful and good that we do not have time to discover that we are not so beautiful and so good. Humility is a strong exercise we have to practise in every moment of our life. It is an exercise which implies some courage. It is also a particularly difficult exercise when we have contradictory feelings – from wishing to be humble to finding it bad to be humble. The progressive teacher, no matter where she or he teaches, in schools or at universities, has to practise humility. I also think that the reactionary teacher would be a better reactionary if she or he were humble. I will illustrate this point. Suppose that a student asks a question which is not very well formulated, a kind of naive question. Then the teacher emphasizes precisely the naivety of the student, and ironically answers as if saying: "Please, first become competent and afterwards come back to ask your question". This is terrible. Possibly this student will never ask another question again, and will never trust the teacher from that moment on. The teacher will have created a barrier making the relationship impossible. The humble teacher also accepts being criticized by the student. She or he can only teach humility through examples. Humility is not something which we can speak about with an absence of humility. I cannot make an arrogant speech to teach humility. This is absolutely impossible.

Another quality which comes together with humility is the ability we have to love. When I say to love I mean to love the very process of teaching; to discover how beautiful it is to be involved in the process of teaching to the extent that the process of teaching is directed towards the process of education, which is rather different from training. Philosophically speaking, training is a very bad word, with very narrow limits in semantics. Educating involves ethics and aesthetics hand in hand; it is beautiful because it is ethical. During the very process of teaching I have to discover that I am inside another process which is the same one which is the process of education. This is beautiful in itself. If I am not able to discover how teaching has to do with beauty, it is not easy for me to love teaching. That is why I said earlier that my point is not about loving students because they are persons, but it is about loving both the object – students – and the process of teaching. The more I do that, the more I discover the need to be humble. It is impossible to think of separating beauty from teaching; beauty from ethics; and the love for students from loving the process through which I must love the students. I love my students not because they are in a room where I am a teacher. I love my students to the extent in which I love the very process of being with them.

The next quality of the progressive teacher is related to the previous one. I should not transform the students into mere shadows of myself. I cannot consider the students as mere objects of the process of teaching where I am the subject. Therefore I have to acknowledge that the students are subjects in the process of learning as well as I am the subject of the process of teaching. However different we – myself and the students – are, students are students, and the teacher is teacher, both students and teacher being the subjects of the process of education. And there is here a contradiction: I cannot teach a subject and have the students as mere objects of my teaching. The students are subjects of their process of learning on the very first day of the academic year. Generally, the students arrive without knowing very clearly that there is something which we name subject or object, given the tradition of the authority of the teacher. I would like to emphasize that I am not saying that the teacher should lose her/ his authority. No! No! No! I do not accept that. What I am trying to say is that the authority of the teacher does not diminish the freedom of the student. One has to grow up through the contradiction of one with the other. In other words, there is no freedom without authority, there is no authority without freedom. It is through the contradictory relationships between authority and freedom that we can experience the value and the need for limits. Without limits there is no possibility for freedom and without limits there is no possibility for authority. What I am saying is that both teacher and students must be subjects of the process of education. In my view to love teaching and to love students is part of the process of developing or helping the development of persons.

Another virtue I now would like very much to emphasize is the virtue or quality of tolerance. This virtue, which is also a political virtue, is very difficult to create. The progressive teacher has to be tolerant. Tolerance is the quality of creating something against certain dimensions of ourselves. It is the ability to enjoy difference. It is to learn from the difference. It means not to consider ourselves better than others precisely because they are different from us. When we think about tolerance we immediately think about racism which is the strongest negation of being tolerant; it is the lowest level of the negation of the differences.

In Brazil, for example, the lack of tolerance concerning political choices is incredible. This is true also inside the universities. That is why I think we have the right to be different from the other. Here I remember the first group of graduate students I had at the Catholic University in São Paulo, coming back from exile in 1980. I had asked the students to write a paper. One of them handed in his paper and said:" I already know that you will not like my paper, and I will be given a low grade". I took the papers home, read them all, and marked them, writing my comments. I easily identified the paper of that student because it was very reactionary. Seriously reactionary. Competently reactionary. He was not lying in the text. He was defending a different position vis-à-vis my position. I gave him ten, the highest grade. I wrote on his paper: "In spite of my total disagreement I gave you ten as a sign of respect for your seriousness, but please try not to be so reactionary". He could not believe it when he saw his mark. I told him: "Look, I did not come here to mark your ideology which I think is horrible, terrible. But I respect you". At that moment I think I gave him something more than a grade of ten. He understood that I was able to have empathy with him, especially because he was antagonistic to me. I think that a teacher who is not able to do that cannot teach; she or he cannot speak about education as an educative process. Nevertheless, the fact of being tolerant does not mean that we have to become indifferent or irresponsible. No. The tolerant teacher tries to understand the weaknesses of the students without however helping them to be weak; she or he challenges the students to be stronger, not to be lazy. The teacher is tolerant when she or he understands the difficulties the students have, and she or he tries to help the students. She or he does not humiliate the students, does not destroy their dreams.

Of course, those qualities I have been talking about have to be created. We have to create them even when we are challenged by the students. We have to come to the classroom with the objective of making the student go beyond us. It is not so easy for the students to overcome the age, the knowledge, and the experience we have. But, from time to time a student asks a question which challenges us in such a way that we do not know very well how to answer. The intolerant teacher will lie in such a situation. The tolerant teacher will have the courage to say: "I am sorry. I do not understand your question. I am not able to answer it today. But I will study it". I never forget, for example, when I was very young and had just begun my teaching career at the university. One day a student asked me a question whose answer I did not know. I said: "Are you free this weekend?" She replied: "Yes, I am". I then said: "I invite you to come to my house, to have lunch with my family, and to spend some time with me in my small study. There I have very good books where I am sure we will be able to answer your question. If you accept my invitation, I will be very happy". She accepted it very eagerly, and we spent the whole Saturday together.[1]

Now, as my final point, I will tell you that one of the issues we face as teachers is the possibility (or not) of creating in ourselves the quality of being consistent and coherent. I think that the first quality – or its absence – the students perceive in a teacher is lack of consistency. For example, how is it possible for a teacher to speak about democracy at the same time as she or he says to the student 'shut up!'. Two absolutely contradictory things. This does not mean that by being democratic she or he has to permit everything. Maybe in some moments as a democratic person you have to say 'shut up'. But, you have to have some conditions in order to say that. For example, when you have to fight. Democratic persons are not prevented from fighting. They have to fight even for democracy. However what is unacceptable is to exercise contradictory values through practice. In other words, to say one thing and to do another. The students will easily perceive the contradiction. I remember when I was living in Geneva where a great friend of mine was at the University of Geneva studying authoritarian regimes. She was quite pleased with the course because the teacher was really very competent. But also very authoritarian. In

— a particular day, the topic was authoritarianism. The teacher discussed it, revealing her position which was against authoritarianism. At a given moment during the lecture my friend took a cigarette out of her bag. Whilst still listening very carefully to the teacher, she started to light the cigarette. The teacher then said, looking at my friend: "Do you know who I am?" What a fantastic question! My friend said that she was so puzzled that she did not grasp immediately the purpose of the question. She thought that the teacher was asking her an absurd question. Her reply was: "Yes, I do, you are the teacher". The teacher says: "How funny. I thought that if you knew who I am you would not even take out a cigarette without my permission". Hearing that, my friend got hold of her books, stood up and said to the teacher who remained silent: "Professor, many thanks for your three lectures. You are very competent, but very contradictory. I am no longer your student because you are a total disappointment." And she left. I wonder how it is possible to speak about democracy, and about freedom with no respect for the freedom of the students. How is it possible to speak about consistency without being consistent?

This case makes me think of a very difficult thing which is to try to combine words and action. Of course, it is impossible to be absolutely consistent. No one is. First, if someone is invariably consistent she or he would not know that she or he is consistent. You can only understand consistency if you experience some degree of inconsistency. Secondly, to be consistent all the time may be a disaster. We must experience some inconsistency within limits, in order to discover the need to be consistent.

My very final point. We must fight for the qualities and virtues I have been talking about. This must be a daily exercise. I am 72 years old. Therefore, my teaching load is not very heavy at the Catholic University. But I am writing a lot. Occasionally I give public lectures in different countries. However I could not do that if I were not, like today, looking for consistency, loving what I do, trying to be humble, controlling my vanity, accepting the differences; it is an exercise for every day. Thank you very much.

NOTE

1. Editorial Note: At this point, someone brought water to Paulo Freire who, thinking it was time to finish his talk, said: "I also have the experience of bureaucratization of time. I always understood schedule as an attempt to command time. But I am the subject of schedule and not the object of it. Last year in December I gave a public lecture in Gothenburg, Sweden, in an international conference. It was not very clear how much time I had for my

paper. At a given moment the organizer, a beautiful woman, very specialized in controlling time, brought me a gift. Puzzled, I asked: 'Is it time for me to stop?' And she said: 'Yes'. Then I replied: 'Of course, I will obey. I will stop because first of all you have the power. But before I stop I have something to say to all of you, and to you, Madam: Yes , I will stop, but I cannot understand why you paid two first class tickets for me and my wife to come from Brazil, so far away from here. You are also paying me a very high fee, and you do not allow me to finish my speech. Nevertheless, as you are paying me, I will stop.'

Nita is just reminding me that the end of my lecture in Sweden was very appropriate because I was speaking about the bureaucratization of the mind. And I added: 'One of the things we should fight against above all in this so-called First World is how we become servants of time which we think we command. How can you put together first class tickets, a high fee and not permit me to finish the speech? How is it possible? You did not understand anything I told you here. Nothing at all. I should be in Brazil, in my house, writing.'

Literacy in Brazil:
The Contribution of Paulo Freire[1]

Ana Maria de Araújo Freire

As Paulo Freire has written:

> The meeting did not take place in a formal hall but in the shade of
> an enormous and very ancient tree. The people demonstrated their
> hospitality by receiving the delegation in the inviting shade of that
> tree, in intimate relation with their own natural world.
>
> My impression was that the shaded area beneath that tree
> was a kind of political-cultural center – a place for informal
> conversation – where they made their work plans together. I also
> thought how such a place, taking advantage of the shade, might be
> used for programs of nonformal education.
>
> As I went toward the tree, admiring its thick foliage, I
> remembered that it had been in the shade of just such trees that
> Amilcar Cabral met with armed militants during the struggle to
> evaluate their action against the colonialist armies. At such times,
> military and tactical analyses never failed to be accompanied by
> political discussions and debates about culture. Through this means
> the permanent leadership squadrons were formed. . .
>
> This was not the false hope of one who hopes for the sake of
> hoping and lives on the basis of vain hope. Hope is true and well
> founded only when it grows out of the unity between action that
> transforms the world and critical reflection regarding the meaning
> of that action. . .
>
> Referring to the violence of the colonialists, one of them bowed
> low and bowed again, curving his body, living the word with which
> he described the terrible treatment received. He walked from one
> side to the other within the circle of shade in which he stood, using
> the movements of his body to express some aspect of the story he
> told. None of them spoke ecstatically, disassociating his body from

*the words he spoke. None spoke only to be heard. In Africa the
word is also to be seen, part of the necessary gesture. No one in
Africa, with the exception of the de-Africanized intellectuals, denies
his roots, or reveals fear or shame in using his body to express his
meaning.*

*And while we saw and heard them speaking, with the force of
their metaphors and the easy movements of their bodies, we thought
of the innumerable possibilities that were opened for a liberating
education by these wellsprings of African culture.*

*They spoke also of the present moment, of their desire to
participate in the struggle for national reconstruction. They spoke,
at the same time, of the difficulties that they confronted.*

*The oldest among them, the one who spoke last in the shade
of that enormous tree, spoke to all of us in the language of hope.*[2]

I come from far away to talk to you about the contribution of Paulo Freire to
literacy in Brazil and I have started my (not so long) talk with words on Africa
that are not mine but Freire's, the Brazilian educationist. From these fragments
of the introduction of **Pedagogy in Process – the Letters To Guinea-Bissau**,
it is possible to understand partially how Paulo Freire feels, thinks, acts and
undertands the words and the world; education, knowledge and society.

In Paulo Freire's language and poetic style, the dialetical thinking, the
scientific rigour, the political commitment, the sensibility for others, and the
effort to re-invent a more just, serious, and democratic world are very much
present. In this re-invented world there is a space for the utopian dream and a
time for hope. In this way Paulo Freire's political-pedagogical-epistemological
thinking is integrated.

The quotation from Paulo Freire can act as the 'generative words' of my
talk on the contribution of Paulo Freire to education in Brazil and in the world,
and not only to literacy.

From this quotation which condenses a large part of Freire's relation to
the world, I would say that Freire is the pedagogue of the obvious, of hope, and
of daring; he is the pedagogue of the verb and of the noun; even more, he is the
pedagogue of thought and of emotion which made him known as the pedagogue
of the oppressed and, hopefully, of the oppressors[3]. Above all, he is the political-
pedagogue, *par excellence*.

Therefore, the Freire quotation permits us to meet *the sensitive man* who,
from his Northeastern origins, values the shade of the big century-old tree which
gives him the pleasure of the fresh breeze and a place to think. We also meet
the man who, intensely concerned with epistemological questions, never forgets,

in the name of scientific knowledge, the question of informal conversation, the expressiveness of 'speaking bodies', the discourse of the 'great man' who possesses the hopeful wisdom of those (traditionally oral) societies; *the political man* who denounces the colonial exploitation which mistreats and violates, who points out, without fear or shame, those cultural sources as the content of a liberating education i. e. the education that makes it possible for men and women to become actors in their history, and from their education to build their truly democratic society; *the pedagogical man* who, from the struggles for a daily life of peace and justice, holds seminars assessing the unity between the transformative action *on* and *of* the world and the critical thinking of hope and of the natural world along with the world of production. The dialectical and utopian themes are clear, and all this is presented with humility and respect.

Paulo Freire has become the political-pedagogue or the pedagogist-politician of the oppressed, of all those who wish to re-invent, from the furnace of colonialism, a just and non-eternally dependent society; of all those so-called minorities (women, blacks, homosexuals, migrants etc.) who need and are willing to participate actively and not marginally, precisely because they have been excluded from the actions of their country and their community; of all those who, suffering from class discrimination, hunger, lack of housing and schools, are unable to name the world because society, closed in its privileges, does not permit them to have; to be; to wish; to know. We wish those people, no matter how they are named – excluded, oppressed or proscribed – to have, to be, to wish, to be able to and to know, and therefore to name the world[4]. To name the world by writing and reading the written word, to name the world by writing and reading in the same world where they live, against the condition of simply *being in* the world rather than *being with* the world, not allowing the patronizing social system to be a weight for them; only through an authentic integration of the "how" and the "through" would they be able to act upon themselves and upon history to re-invent their society.

Freire sketched these things in his first publication – **Education, the Practice for Freedom** – the pedagogue of criticism of Brazilian colonialism and of its consequences, men and women submerged in a society of anti-dialogue, of authoritarianism, of silence, and hierarchy of submission and awareness of (unwelcome) oppression.

Freire's critical – and incipient political – counsciousness emerged from the century-old presence of Brazilian illiteracy exposed atrociously in the streets. His closeness to the illiterate population in Recife, during the 40s and 50s, when he worked in the Educational Division of SESI (Social Service for Industry), led him to think seriously about a solution for one of the biggest Brazilian problems: widespread illiteracy.

The search for a solution to this problem was based on an understanding of the dialetical dichotomy, the subjectivity-objectivity of being in the world, later one of the most remarkable features of Freirian pedagogy. Freire started from a concrete fact, the history of his life in a given period of difficult times in Brazil – the period of the American Economic Depression. After the fall in the New York Stock Exchange, monopolistic capitalism re-structured itself, with perverse consequences for the Third World.

The child Paulo, confined to the small town of Jaboatão, 18 km from Recife, faced pain, suffering and anxiety. He also learned, mysteriously, that he needed to find pleasure for life, love as a principle, and intellectual growth as a necessity.

Freire was framed by daily financial and material difficulties. Nevertheless he had the opportunity to go to one of the best schools in Recife – the Colégio Oswaldo Cruz whose owner was my father, Aluizio Pessoa de Araújo. Struggling through, and working hard, Freire became initiated into scientific knowledge, with special attention devoted to the Portuguese language.

Later, as a teacher in SESI, working with adults, Freire built up his teaching around his difficulties in life and his previous theoretical knowledge about education. From this praxis with the urban, rural and coastal workers, Freire invented a new theory of knowledge – and there is no neutral theory of knowledge – re-creating a new road for those who wished to write.

It was then that he started asking questions: what for, for whom, against whom, how, until when, on behalf of whom, on behalf of what? It was a moment of clarification of the contradictions of the Brazilian economic and political system. He then understood the meaning and the strength of the ideologies he was familiar with.

It was then that Freire understood with clarity that to teach adults how to write and to memorise mechanically the articulation of letters, syllables and words would not give to them the chance to name, speak and decide. They would become permanently, as they have been in Brazil, an object without voice, and passive listeners of norms and orders from 'superiors'.

For Freire, literacy had to have a wider meaning. It had to give men, women and children the opportunity to become actors and not only objects of their history, of their life, of becoming literate in the real act of knowledge which is teaching-learning.

That is why I can say that Freire is the pedagogue of the obvious, of hope and of daring, of objectivity and of subjectivity, of the noun, of the verb, and of the preposition. And of the oppressed because, starting from the reality historically characterised by oppression, Freire created the necessary conditions to overcome it with his liberating pedagogy.

Freire, as a political-pedagogue, was then able to invent a 'method' which, teaching how to write and to read through words and sentences, would make people politically aware.

The way Freire chose to make Brazilians literate was then, as he himself calls it, an educative tactic, in order to reach the necessary and intended strategy, i.e., the political awareness of the Brazilian people. The concept of his 'method' is revolutionary, but it is a revolution in which the tactics and the strategy deny the military and guerrilla meanings. It is revolutionary because it is able to withdraw from a condition of submission and passivity those who did not know the written words. That is where Freire's revolution is, one which never claimed to invert the pole, oppressed-oppressor; on the contrary, what Freire had in mind was to re-invent a society without exploitation and without the verticality of authority.

The birth of this 'method' – I have been raising this thesis as a result of my analysis of Freire's thinking in the History of Brazilian Education – took place, I am sure, when, as the Pernambuco Rapporteur of the Second National Conference of Adult Education, Freire presented new proposals to one of the themes put forward by the then Minister of Education Clovis Salgado who had called for the Conference: "Adult Education and the marginalised population: shanty-towns, huts, slums and communities of foreigners" (Theme 3).

This Conference took place from 6 to 16 July 1958, when President Juscelino Kubitscheck, fully in power, wanted to solve the problems of poverty and lack of education within the frame of the populist ideology. However the ideas, the discourse and the practice of Paulo Freire already indicated the road to an authentic popular pedagogy.

Such concerns within the political society met those of part of the civilian society in the fifties. There was an appropriate ambiance for mobilisation, for thinking and the will for social and political changes.

These progressive components of the civilian society – urban and rural workers, students, university teachers, intellectuals and the catholic clergy – were no longer willing to accept the *status quo* but wanted to break with the archaic, authoritarian, discriminatory and elitist traditions which had dominated Brazil for centuries.

Many were those among the politicians who thought and tried to search for solutions towards development. Some elements of the civilian society resented poverty, social injustice and the widespread illiteracy among the Brazilian people. Freire was one of them and soon became the pedagogue of this resentment.

In the Second Conference of Adult Education, Freire then proposed, in his particular language, within his innovative and progressive philosophy of education, that adult education in the marginal areas be based on the consciousness of the reality lived daily by those to be literated, rejecting the simple process of literacy (later he used to say: simple bla bla blas).

In the Conference Report, Freire proposed that the adult literacy process no longer takes place *upon* (vertically) or *for* (in a patronizing way) men, but *with* men, *with* learners, and *with* reality. Only that way would it be possible to educate for democracy. It is worthwhile to notice that in the fifties and even after the publication, in the seventies, in the USA, of **Pedagogy of the Oppressed**, Freire did not mention women; the word 'men' was understood in its wider sense i.e. human beings.

Freire proposed an adult education that would stimulate collaboration, decision, participation, and social and political responsibility.

Freire took the category of knowledge, which is acquired existentially, through the living knowledge of his problems and those of the local community, knowledge which is not acquired intellectually or notionally. By so doing, Freire made explicit his respect for popular knowledge, for common sense.

As Rapporteur of the Pernambuco Commission of Theme 3, Freire anticipated some aspects of his understanding of the world which became deeper twelve years later in **Pedagogy of the Oppressed**, after several experiences in Brazil and abroad, including his condition of political exile. The issue of the oppressed was with him since he was a child in Jaboatão, when he felt it through the homes and streets of Brazil.

The Report talked about social education, about pupils knowing themselves and their social problems, and was not only concerned about acquiring academic and technical abilities. It stimulated people to participate in the immersion process of public life. Freire emphasised that it was the learners' duty to plan the content of their studies. He also stimulated pedagogical work in the slums and pointed out that women overcome their condition of destitution by changing the nature of their domestic practices.

Such a philosophy of education contained already a clear perception of the discriminatory routine of our mainly patriarchal and elitist society. Freire presented solutions to overcome these conditions, ahead of time, within a broader and more progressive conception: education as a political act. All that was very new in Brazil which used to exclude through social reproduction those who are socially disadvantaged[5].

I am sure that in that Second Conference Paulo Freire created in the history of Brazilian education a new concept of adult education. He has contributed, since then, to a real critical undertanding of illiteracy, and of the act of educating. He was also very perceptive about the political nature of education.

The political nature of education, even before its pedagogical, technical and didactic specificity, has been Freire's main concern, not only in his theoretical thinking but also in his educative praxis.

Since then, Freire has been shaping himself according to his experience as the pedagogue of the oppressed – even before writing his book **Pedagogy of the Oppressed** – because he based it on popular knowledge and language, on people's dreams, respecting their reality and their daily lives. Above all, he extended these thoughts into a proposal to overcome this world of submission, of silence and poverty, and to move towards a world of possibilities.

Freire 'invites' the adults who are learning how to read and write to consider themselves as men or women living and producing in a particular society. He removes the illiterates from the apathy and conformity which constantly make them regard themselves as individuals who have been 'sacked from life'. Freire challenges them to understand that they are also taking part in the process of creating culture. He teaches them the anthropological concept of culture.

Freire based his 'method' on a simple and obvious principle: when a man transforms clay into brick in order to build his house, he is at the same time producing culture, aware that he knows what he is doing. He also should be able to use words to build sentences, to use syllables to build words. He is therefore capable of acquiring reading and writing skills, because men and women are capable of expressing their spoken language in a written code.

The fact of belonging to a less privileged social class has to be seen not as a divine wish or fate but as part of the economic-political-ideological context of the society in which they live. They will be unveiling the true reasons for oppression.

When these men and women notice that they have active roles in the process of creating their own culture, they will have almost or totally overcome the first stage to perceiving the importance, the need, and the possibility of acquiring reading and writing skills. They will be learning how to read and write, from a political point of view.

The participants of the 'circles of culture' answer the questions formulated by the group coordinator, in a dialogue about the topic to be learned, the representation of reality, and the written words to be decoded. They are learning how to read and write, politically as much as linguistically, in an inseparable and dialectical process.

Such a dialogue allows for a re-evaluation of reality which can result in getting the individual who is learning how to read and write involved with the political practices that can lead to the transformation of society and, consequently, to its re-invention.

What? Why? How? What for? Whom for? Against what? Against whom?

In favour of what? In favour of whom? These questions, I repeat, stimulate these learners to reflect about the essence of things that surround them, their importance, their reason, their purpose, how they are made, and so on. Through a pedagogy of questioning, Freire ensures that answers would result from the consciousness of learners.

The activities involved in teaching how to read and write require the study of what Freire calls the 'minimum vocabulary universe' amongst the learners. The words that will be part of the programme will be chosen from this universe. These words (approximately seventeen), which are called 'generative words', should be phonemically rich, and should be presented in an ascending order of phonetic difficulty. In addition, these words should be selected from the context of the learners' daily lives, they should be used by the local community and should be known by those who live and work there. These words should have a pragmatic value for the men and women who are learning how to read and write[6].

When these learners are able to articulate syllables to form words and sentences, then they know how to read and write. The process has to be appropriately developed.

The effectiveness and validity of the 'method' resides, then, in the fact that it is based on the learners' reality, on what they already know, on the pragmatic value of the things and facts of their daily lives, and on their living conditions. Freire surpasses common sense and becomes the pedagogue of the obvious, of the people, and of hope.

The 'method' abides by methodological and linguistic norms, but it goes beyond them. It challenges the men and the women who are learning how to read and write to seize the written code and its political meaning, providing a widespread notion not only of language, but also of the world, as a true political-linguistic pedagogue must do.

The 'method' denies the merely alienated and alienating repetition of words and syllables, it allows the learners 'to read the world' as well as 'to read the word'. As a matter of fact, according to Freire, these are inseparable readings. Readings in accord with the needs of the people.

In brief, this work of Paulo Freire is more than a 'method' of teaching how to read and write. It consists of a wide and deep understanding of education, whose main concern is the political nature of education and of the world.

This pedagogy of challenge, of curiosity, and of the obvious is made for those who were not allowed to read and write either the word and the world.

Since the **Pedagogy of the Oppressed**, the work that made Paulo Freire renowned as a world figure, Freire's thoughts became more and more political.

However, Freire, coherently and correctly, never abandoned his pedagogical thinking.

With his dialogic action theory, Freire proposed the liberation 'weapons' of collaboration, union, organisation, and cultural synthesis as elements antagonistic to the anti-dialogue, which it would oppose. This anti-dialogue has characterised Brazil since the sixteenth century, when it was conquered by the Portuguese, until today.

According to dialogic action theory, people collaborate with one another in order to transform the world, revealing, by cultural action, why and how the oppressed are bonded to the reality. This bondage leads to a false self-awareness and a false knowledge of their reality which is hidden by the ideology. That is why it is so important to reverse this process. As far as organisation is concerned, the necessary instruments would be leadership, no matter what kind, discipline, order, objectives, tasks to be carried out and results to be reported. One cannot be totally relaxed; there is need for authentic authority. It is important to encourage a cultural synthesis against the invasion that annihilates the oppressed with its ideological and valuational milestones.

Hence, Freirean thought became increasingly influenced by an authentic dialogicity which creates, recreates, educates, and humanises through the pedagogy of dialogue. It is a pedagogy that dares and takes risks, unveils, raises curiosity for knowledge, and tolerates. It asks and answers, transforms ingenuity into criticism, establishes rules from common sense, gives responsibilities and authority. This pedagogy aims at clarity and at being part of a political dream. It denies the extremes of spontaneity and authoritarianism, and makes the learning process a surprising one, stimulating creativity and an unpretentious capability as well as coherence between what is said and what is done. In addition, it stimulates trust in oneself and in others. In sum, this pedagogy, which is based on daily life experience, pursues theory to shed light on to the practice that grants freedom.

Freire's political pedagogy, which above all denies authoritarianism, discrimination, and elitism that have been entrenched in Brazilian society for a long time, is based on the patience of the impatient, on humbleness, on rebelliousness, on militancy, on commitment and organisation, on debate, on fight, on conflict and dialogue, on political compromise, on justice and awareness, on human interest and dignity, on totality, on contradiction and on the concrete reality of men, women and the world. It strengthens the cry that comes from the people in order to make it a cry of indignation and hope, instead of an empty cry which neither expresses purpose nor grants power to people. Thus, Freire has become more and more radical in his position as the political pedagogue of the oppressed.

Until this moment, I have been talking, apparently, only about Freire's qualitative contribution not only to the teaching of reading and writing, but also, and more widely, to the process of educating as a whole. It is quite difficult to talk strictly about the quantitative data that came direct or indirectly from his work. The official statistical data do not show everything, because after the coup d'état of 1964 they have been ideologically manipulated. The popular education movements have not registered the data appropriately. However, the data from the Municipal Secretariat of Education of São Paulo will be extremely valuable for this analysis, when compared to those from administrations before and after Freire's. I should add that to distinguish quantity from quality is certainly not the best option from the scientific-methodological-political point of view, because quantity implies quality, and vice-versa.

I believe, though, that I have to point out Freire's different and more important practices from the sixties onwards, in Brazil. I must also say that these practices cannot be dissociated from the theory that enlightened them.

With his knowledge of education, Freire cooperated in the creation of the Cultural Extension Service (*Serviço de Extensão Cultural*) in the then University of Recife, when the education radio service was launched. He, then, systematised his literacy 'method' in the same university where he was a lecturer in History and Philosophy of Education.

Together with other intellectuals and ordinary people, he founded the Popular Culture Movement (*Movimento de Cultura Popular*) of Recife, where he first used his 'literacy method'. He helped the Literacy Campaign in the city of Natal, in the State of Rio Grande do Norte, called 'Barefoot people can also learn how to read'(*De pé no chão também se aprende a ler*). Freire led the same type of campaign in the town of Angicos, when he became known in the whole country and in outside world as the creator of the 'consciousness raising literacy method'.

When the first class of students from this small town in Rio Grande do Norte completed the course, President João Goulart attended the graduation ceremony. Freire was then invited to coordinate a national campaign which was called the National Literacy Programme. It was intended to teach 5 million illiterate adults, which would increase considerably the number of electors. The programme, officially created on the 22nd of January 1964, in order to implement the plan elaborated by the Popular Culture Commission on the 8th of July 1963, was also coordinated by Freire, and was almost immediately cancelled, when on the 13th of April 1964 the Commission was abolished by a decree from the new military government.

The sixteen years of exile were responsible for his silence and his absence from Brazil, because he and his ideas were forbidden in his country. He wandered around the world, as he likes to put it, and became a pedagogue of the world.

When he returned to Brazil in 1980, Freire became even more radical in his classes at universities – in the Pontifical Catholic University of São Paulo (PUC/SP) or in the University of Campinas (UNICAMP), where he has lectured until 1990. He also participated in seminars at these institutions and in a number of other popular organisations, reinforcing his position that education is a theory of knowledge put into practice and that it is possible to establish that knowledge, being a historical process, results from the conscious practice of men and women, who are aware of their time and space, of their objective reality which, in turn, makes them part of the historical dialectic process that makes history.

Freire states that in education, as a result of a certain theory of knowledge put into practice, it is necessary, I repeat, to raise questions about the content – the object to be explored – about the learning 'method' and the evaluation of this practice, and, under no circumstances, to abandon the concrete reality of the learners.

Furthermore, since this content, this 'method', and this evaluation are located in a particular time and are put into practice within a certain space, they are historical. As such, they are aimed at real people who, in the process of teaching and learning, need not only to acquire knowledge, as a consequence of what they have memorised, but also to use it for their own good as well as that of their society. They can reinvent life and make history, the same history that they have always been part of.

Freire accepted his nomination as Secretary of Education of the City of São Paulo, and on the 1st of January 1989 he was inaugurated. This happened because the Workers' Party (*Partido dos Trabalhadores*), of which he is one of the founders, won the elections for the São Paulo City Council with Luiza Erundina de Souza as Mayor.

In his highly democratic administration, he proved that consensus and collegial work can lead to collective responsibility and to the re-creation of the educative process itself more efficiently and adequately.

His political decisions were born out of his own theory and out of his practice as an educationalist *for* the world – indeed, *of* the world – as well as out of the educational praxis of his technical advisers with whom he worked, who reflected the wishes and needs of the communities. Such political decisions were remarkably infuential in the educational system of the municipality of São Paulo.

Thus, 'his' (and his team's) work was fruitful in the sense of 'changing the face of the school', as he usually says. He transformed the schools by bringing them back to the local communities, and by providing them with the necessary conditions for the exercise of pedagogical activities. He reformulated the curriculum, giving to it a new orientation and adjusting it to children of the lower classes. He also encouraged staff development within a perspective of permanent training. He did not forget to include ancillary staff as educational agents, providing them with training in order to improve their performance. Security guards, cooks, cleaners, secretaries, together with principals, teachers, pupils, and their parents transformed education into a collaborative act of ellaborated knowledge. Education, then, originated from the social needs felt by and for the community and to the world, having as mediators both the school, its agents, and the technical equipment.

Having left the Municipal Secretary of Education of São Paulo before his term of office ended – he carried on being a member of the Secretariat Collegiate until the end of 1992 – he left public life to be 'given back to the world', as the Mayor of São Paulo, Luiza Erundina, said at his farewell party, in the Municipal Theatre of São Paulo, in May 27, 1991. Since then, he has been devoting himself to his lifetime activity: writing, lecturing, and talking to people.

This is true. In the last two years Freire wrote three books. This morning we have had him here at the Institute of Education of the University of London to talk about education, and about how he sees his political-pedagogical thinking. This institution is also opening its doors to me so that I can tell you a bit about the researches I have been engaged in, regarding Paulo Freire's influences in the history of Brazilian education. This influence has been an important part of the history of the political-pedagogical ideas of the Brazilian nation. Ideas and practices with a worldwide influence, as if to confirm one of the key ideas of the Freirean thought: nobody knows everything and nobody ignores everything.

It is the Third World which, having learned from the First World, is contributing to a new understanding of a world desired by all of us, from everywhere. A new world, more egalitarian, fairer and more democratic to all men, women and children of the so called North, South, East and West.

Like one of the 'great men' of Africa, Paulo Freire learned with men and women of Africa, Asia and the Americas. Literate or illiterate, powerful or powerless men and women, but above all men and women with souls and the weaknesses of those who have nothing and 'know nothing'. Above all, he has been learning from the suffering Brazilian people, who have been neglected for centuries.

Paulo Freire has become the pedagogue of de-mystification. Because of what he has relentlessly been, and has been doing for nearly all his life, with no pessimism, but actively and hopefully. Because he understood like nobody else the dialectics opressor-opressed, which he wishes to see overcome and which the world, in surprise and astonishment, has been admitting with humility. This is, with no doubt, his greatest contribution not just to Brazil, but to the whole world.

Thank you very much.

NOTES

1. Translated by Terezinha Benevides Lobianco, Monica Pereira dos Santos and Maria de Figueiredo-Cowen.

2. Freire, Paulo. *Pedagogy in process – the letters to Guinea-Bissau.* London: Writers and Readers Publishing Cooperative, 1978. pp.59-62.

3. Editors' Note. The author talks here through metaphors which are related to grammatical categories. The pedagogue of the verb is here understood as the pedagogue of action (to learn, to teach, to love, to think, to do) whilst the pedagogue of the noun is the pedagogue of the essence.

   In addition the author uses the word 'obvious' to mean all that is intuitively understood. The pedagogue of the obvious is the pedagogue who rethinks the obvious relations in education, challenging what is taken for granted.

4. See Freire, Ana Maria A. *Analfabetismo no Brasil (1534-1930)* [Illiteracy in Brazil]. São Paulo: Cortez, 1989.

5. Editors' Note. Ana Maria Freire uses in the Portuguese text the expression 'proscription of bodies' to mean the colonial ideology of exclusion dating back to the colonial acts of the Portuguese and Catholic Church in the 16th century. Proscription in Portuguese is a stronger expression than prohibition. The native Indians, the blacks and the women were excluded from participation in society during colonial times. They were considered inferior human beings.

6. See Freire, P. *Education, the practice of freedom.* London: Writers and Readers Publishing Cooperative, 1976.

   Editors' Note. This book was first published in the UK under the title: *Education for critical consciousness.* London: Sheed and Ward, 1974.

Discussing Paulo Freire:

Representation as Transformation

Gunther Kress

Anyone who is engaged in education is involved in the process of transformation; and so the larger questions which Paulo Freire has raised in his political project are questions for any educator. Education is always **for** something. Even when education is education for conformity, there is an assumption of a human being who must be educated to conform, who would not otherwise do so. Education is always a **prospective** enterprise: **for** a future, namely the future in which these small and young human beings now in this classroom, will be living their adult social lives – productively, we hope. Education, for most of us, is therefore a utopian enterprise, an attempt to make available to this group of young humans the means whereby they can engage in the process of transformation which will allow them to lead productive lives in that imagined future which is the goal of education.

I work in a small area of this large project, namely that which has to do with the making of meaning through outwardly visible means, the area currently and fashionably known by the term 'literacy' in Anglophone countries. This is the area that attempts to understand the incessant enterprise of making and remaking of representations of ourselves for ourselves, of ourselves for others; attempts to understand, in these processes of representation, who we are, what this place around us is; but attempts also to project other possibilities, of who we might be, and what this place around us could or should be.

The processes of representation, and the means available to us for making representation, are **central** in attempts to sustain or alter or remake our dreams. The means of representation are therefore, in my view, central in any attempts aimed at the transformation of our culture, and of our world. As an educator, with a utopian goal, my concern is with an understanding of these transformational means, and an understanding of how they may be made available to those who will need these means in order to play their part in transforming their world in the direction of **their** dreams.

This is where my interest in literacy connects with Paulo Freire's educational and political project. To use a phrase of his: "I become, by doing what I intend to become". My domain of "doing" is the domain of making representations of the world; in this doing, we transform our subjectivities. My academic, intellectual project has been that of a critical rethinking, a remaking of theories of language, and of representation, under the labels of Critical Linguistics (C.L.) and Critical Discourse Analysis (C.D.A.). These have, from the beginning, had a political project: broadly speaking that of altering inequitable distributions of economic, cultural and political goods in contemporary societies. The intention of this has been to bring a system of excessive inequalities of power into crisis by uncovering its workings and its effects through the analysis of potent cultural objects – texts, and thereby help in achieving a more equitable social order. The central issue of CDA has thus been one of transformation: unsettling the existing order, and transforming its elements into an arrangement less harmful to some, perhaps more beneficial to all the members of a society. In the process the various critical language projects have developed an impressive range of analytic/critical procedures, and have provided, in the analyses developed, clear insights into the social, political and ideological processes at work.

In this, it has become essential to take two decisive steps: one, towards the articulation of the theory of language, of communication, of semiosis, which is implied in these critical language activities: to develop an apt theory of language as a part of an apt theory of semiosis.

The second is closely related. Critical language projects must move from critical reading, from analysis, from deconstructive activity, to productive activity. Uncovering inequitable, dehumanizing states of affairs is crucial: developing means of enabling humans to act as agents of transformation and production of new, more equitable social arrangements is central.

If linguistic, cultural, economic resources are at present unequally distributed along the lines of class, gender, age, profession, ethnicity, race, region, etc. with the consequent formations of subjectivities (one might say deformations, in relation to what might be) then it behoves critical language projects, I believe, to begin to turn their attention to this enterprise. It may be that my present professional location in education forces this view on me with particular urgency. My job requires of me that I think about and concern myself with the school-curriculum, specifically the English curriculum. A curriculum is a design for a future social subject, and via that envisioned subject a design for a future society. That is, the curriculum puts forward knowledges, skills, meanings, values in the present which will be telling in the lives of those who experience the curriculum, ten or twenty years later. Forms of pedagogy experienced by children now in school suggest to them forms of social relations which they are encouraged to adopt, adapt, modify, treat as models. The curriculum, and its associated pedagogy, puts forward a set of cultural, linguistic, social resources which students have available as resources for their own transformation; in relation to which (among others) students constantly construct, reconstruct, transform their subjectivity.

Such a view of the curriculum and of pedagogy requires however (though this seems not, in Britain at least, the common assumption) that those who construct the curriculum have a vision of the future in which this human being, here and now experiencing the curriculum, will lead her or his life, as a culturally, personally, socially productive life. It behoves me therefore to state my vision of that future in relation to which I imagine the curriculum. My span of prediction is about 20 years: a period at the end of which a child now entering school will be about 25 years old. I want to have a part in the construction of a positive future, and so I imagine a society which has been willing to deal with several fundamental issues: the issue of multiculturalism first and foremost; the issue of appropriately productive forms of sociality; the issues of the economy and of technology in an age which will be even more deeply transnational than our present period is; and by no means last, the issues arising out of the massive technological and economic transformations of what used to be called the mass media.

My vision therefore focuses on the kind of curriculum – its contents, as well as the form in which its contents are made available – which will be essential in achieving such a vision. More than that, however, I focus on the kind of human subject required to carry this task of acting in that society, to make it productive in personal, cultural, social, economic ways. My concern is to imagine what resources the curriculum needs to make available to children who are now in schools in order for them to be able to achieve for themselves that task of transformation. I imagine that the citizen of the society of twenty years hence will have to be confident in the face of difference of all kinds and to see difference as a major personal, cultural, economic resource; that they will have to be at ease with constant and continuing change.

In my view the set of representational resources and the practices associated with each of these, that is, the (formal) means and practices by which we represent ourselves to ourselves and to others, play an absolutely crucial role in the formation of an individual's subjectivity. On the one hand these are the resources which are available to an individual as the means whereby she or he can effect the transformation of her or his subjectivity, to produce a particular habitus. On the other hand, the representational resources are not highly plastic, that is, they represent, in the content of their form, rich social histories. The media of representation (eg language, whether written or spoken; the visual, whether as painting, drawing, photography; the gestural, etc) have inherent possibilities and limitations as media of representation and communication. That is, the representational resources constitute a highly specific technology, among other things, which are enabling in certain directions, and which impede in others.

One essential and urgent task in a multicultural society is therefore to conduct an ethnography of representational resources, across all the major, identifiable groups in a society. This ethnography would include descriptions of social valuations which attach to the representational resources used by various groups. Such a description would be accompanied by a semiotic analysis of these resources, and of the media of representation through which they were realized.

So for instance, in the domain of language, it will be important to know the semiotic potential of the grammars used by all the ethnic/linguistic groups in a society; to know the characteristic forms of text of all the groups; to know, for instance, what valuations attach to speech as against writing; and to know also how this distinction is articulated and valued. Beyond language, one would want to know about all the other media of public communication which the various groups in a society have at their disposal, and what meanings are characteristically carried by these, with greater or lesser ease, and with what social recognition, valuation, and effect.

In this view the issue of equity for instance, takes on a quite specific character: whereas until now equity has been seen as a matter of making concessions to marginal groups, allowing them access to goods which the dominant or mainstream group(s) enjoy, of being 'nice' to those less fortunate than oneself, it will, rather, have to be treated as a matter which works reciprocally, in **all** directions. A truly equitable society is one in which the groups with greater access to economic, cultural, political goods see it as essential to have access to the linguistic and cultural resources of minority groups, and will recognize this need for access to these goods as a matter of equity for them, and for society at large. Equity cannot be left as a matter of making concessions; it has to be seen as a matter of equality of cultural trade, where each social group is seen as having contributions of equal value to make to all other social groups in the larger social unit.

But for that to be a possibility, we need precisely that inventory of the larger linguistic, semiotic, cultural, social economy. We need to know with great precision what are "the myriad of mundane processes of training and learning . . . which literally mould the body and become second nature" (Thompson, 1992). My assumption is that the potentials in the processes of representation – how cultural groups and their individual members can and do represent themselves, what kinds of representations they receive – are likely to be crucial in the inculcation of representational 'table manners', and are crucial in moulding social bodies.

Here I wish to do no more than provide some brief illustrative descriptions. These are meant to be no more than suggestive: my purpose is to indicate what I regard as an essential issue for a critical language project to address. It will be plain however that there is one further fundamental challenge to present thinking about representation, and communication. I do not believe that it is any longer possible to give adequate accounts of texts, even of texts which appear in the print media (let alone those which appear on television, or in cinemas) without transcending, decisively, the hitherto relatively rigorously observed "boundaries" of the verbal medium. All texts have always been multi-modal, that is, are always, have always been constituted through a number of semiotic modes. The current period is one where this is now impossible to overlook: not only because the visual is so visible, but also because I wish to suggest that we are in the centre of a major historical move in so-called technologically developed (western) societies which is re-ordering the public, social weighting of the various media of expression. The visual is becoming increasingly dominant, as the verbal is becoming less dominant in many areas of public communication – and this is not simply the effect of technology. Indeed I would wish to say that it is the effect of much larger social forces, of which multi-culturalism is one significant one.

In Paulo Freire's notion of social transformations, he considers two agents of transformation: the teacher, and the learner. The latter is seen as the agent of her or his self-transformation, using the means which the teacher has made available for the learner in this process. This makes the learner active and agentive in relation to this formation of their own subjectivity. I wish to extend this description by one crucial addition: the learner transforms not only his or her subjectivity, but transforms the representational resources which she or he uses in that process of self-transformation.

Allow me to explain using an example. Below is a drawing by a three-year old boy, which he himself named: "This is a car". For the three-year old this **is** a car by a complex metaphoric process, in which circles are, in criterial respects, like wheels; and wheels are, in criterial respects, the defining characteristic of **car**.

The example allows me to make two points: one about the motivated nature of the sign; and the other about the matter of **interest**. This complex sign, the drawing **car**, is a motivated sign, deriving its motivation from the "interest" of the three-year old. It is the motivation of signs which allows us to read back, hypothetically, to the interest of the producer of the sign, however complex that interest may be. That interest is a direct consequence and expression of the sign-maker's subjectivity – focused in this instance and at the moment of representation on a particular (aspect of an) object or event. Wheels are, clearly, focal in the child's "interest" in cars. Through the signmaker's interest a transformation is achieved, a metaphor is established, which transforms the (represented) world at the moment when it is brought into semiosis.

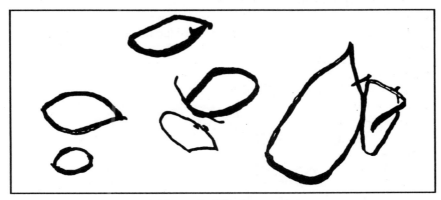

Figure 1 'This is a car'

The history of the child's own development of the representational resources which led him to the production of the sign of the car is relatively well recoverable; and here are some markers along that micro-historical path. This achievement of circles

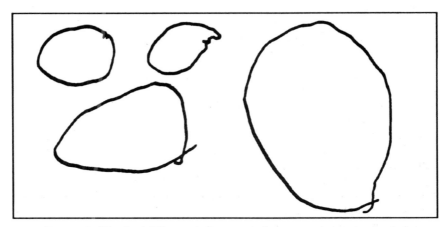

Figure 2 'Circles' (These circles were drawn on separate sheets)

underpinned his ability to produce the representation of the car. That is, as he developed a particular representational resource, the circle, it enabled him to move to a further level of representational capacity, in producing the more complex sign of the car. The production of the representational resources, the changed possibilities of him as a subject in relation to the world, in this case representing/transforming the world, seems strongly evident to me. Even earlier stages are recoverable, when the signs produced were quite different – when, perhaps, expression as gesture, and formal production are very closely inter-related.

Figure 3 'Circular gestures'

My point is one about the reciprocal relations between subjectivity; the subject's production of representational resources; the transformation by the subject of his subjectivity via the newly produced representational resources; the transformative power of the subject in and on the world as a consequence of this prior transformation; and the subject's renewed transformation of the representational resources. In this instance the process is perhaps particularly clear because it is **relatively** free of the cultural and the social forms of representation; though it is of course the social and cultural world itself which has prompted this sequence of production.

Transformation by the subject of her or his subjectivity in relation to the available representational resources is my central point. **Interest** is for me a category that allows me to express the momentary focusing, condensation, of subjectivity, the response to the whole host of contingent social factors and past histories which accompany the making of signs. **Interest** has of course been a central concern in Freire's political project; and the starting point of his pedagogy.

I will take a huge metaphoric step and move to a discussion of a series of images, all of them the front-pages of newspapers. My first example is the front page of the *Frankfurter Allgemeine*: a somewhat unusual newspaper now in Western Europe (though *Le Monde* is quite similar in one respect) in its continued insistence on the prominence of the representational resource of verbal language.

All texts are multi-semiotic and here I will focus on aspects of layout, on typographical features (eg densely spaced print, use of certain type-faces to distinguish genres, for instance **report** from **opinion**; the length of items, and so on). The typographical and layout features are, broadly, homologous with this paper's insistence on the dominance of the verbal: the dense spacing suggests a reader who can and will take the time, make the effort, have the concentration to read this text. The length of items suggests that this is a reader who would not wish to be 'short-changed', who wishes to have a serious treatment of an issue. The use of different typeface – and the gothic typeface, with its suggestion of (temporal) distance – suggests the wish to be clear about signalling the ontological status of the different genres. In short, this set of semiotic features, of representational resources, suggests and implies, and I would wish to say, over the longer term **produces**, a particular disposition, a particular habitus and, in so doing, plays its part in the production of a particular kind of subjectivity, a subjectivity with certain orientations to 'rationality'. (Freire's: "We never are, we become", and "I become, by doing what I intend to become" – except that here this intention may be skewed "I become what someone else intends that I become").

The newspaper front page shown is a facsimile of the *Frankfurter Allgemeine Zeitung für Deutschland* with headlines including "Moskau droht mit der „Liquidierung der bewaffneten Formationen" in Tschetschenien", "Absolute Mehrheit für Bulgariens Sozialisten", and "Generalstabschefs der Nato beraten über Unprofor".

Courtesy of the *Frankfurter Allgemeine* Newspaper

Figure 4. Frankfurter Allgemeine (FA)

Clearly, this newspaper speaks to, and is read by, a particular kind of reader. It would be an entire mistake to treat these aspects as merely formal, as marginal, as not of the core of the matter. On the contrary I would say that it is these formal matters as much as the 'lexis' of the front-page which characterise this particular reader/subject (as well as the producer/subject). Features such as these sustain this subjectivity, as well as having their part in forming it. Even though the reciprocal effect between representational resources and subjectivity seems highly static, conservative, its transformative potential on the world and on the reading subject cannot be overestimated. The effort required to attempt to keep the world as it is, the mythic/ideological effort required day after day to maintain a stasis, is every bit as enormous as the efforts required to change the world. The semiotic as well as the political lesson here is that conservatism is an energetic enterprise.

The habitual reader of the *Frankfurter Allgemeine* is happy and comfortable with this paper precisely because there is a broad homology between the structure of the subjectivity of the reader, and the semiotic organisation of this text. It is, for him or her, a reader-friendly publication: even though it may not be our preferred notion of friendliness.

If we move, by contrast, to an English tabloid, *The Sun*, we are met by quite different representational resources: the prominence of the verbal has gone, or rather, it has been fundamentally transformed into 'display' rather than 'information' in the traditional sense. Language has become, largely, a visual element. The very large photograph is in this sense, self-explanatory: that is, it signals directly the prominence of the visual in this paper. Language in the conventional sense is a minor, a nearly insignificant element. The introduction of colour is of course significant: rigorously avoided by the *FA* (though not, for instance, by the *Suddeutsche Zeitung*, which has small elements of colour: a sign of a transformation in progress), but it too signals a shift in the projected subjectivity of the reader. This is a reader, so the organization of the representational resources imply, who does not have the time, the skill, the concentration or willingness to read in a focused fashion. This is a reader who must get her or his perceptions immediately, directly. Information must be presented in a pleasurable fashion – hence the image, and hence particularly the colour.

It may be that the appearance of colour signals particularly strongly the shift in the implied and projected subject – the move from rationality, information, and work to entertainment, pleasure and leisure. Whereas the *FA* usually has about 12 textual items on its front page, *The Sun* has one. Here too lies a huge difference. The resources with which the world is approached, which are available for the transformation of the world, are fundamentally different.

Courtesy of *The Sun* Newspaper

Figure 5. The Sun

The Sun is (nearly) totally synthetic: there is one account of what the world is today; the *FA* by comparison is analytic: there is a multiplicity of accounts of what the world is. This positions or constructs the reader's subjectivity in a radically different fashion. The transformative potential of the representational resources in each case is different. In the case of *The Sun*, synthesis at the 'lexical' ("what the world is about") level precludes, nearly, the possibility of transformation through analysis – though I leave out of account here the issue of the appearance of two distinct semiotic modes and their distinctive representations of content, and of the effect of that. In the case of the *FA*, analysis at the semiotic level (layout, typographical features) is combined with analysis at the lexical level. At best (and this is clearly said from a particular social, political, and moral view) analysis at the semiotic level (the verbal, the visual, colour) in *The Sun* is combined with synthesis at the lexical level: the reader is given fewer resources for analysis and therefore fewer resources for critique.

I wish to pause here just for a moment, to reflect again on the question of representational resources, their potentialities and limitations, and their effects on subjectivity. It seems to me that radically different resources are employed in the two cases; radically different transformative potentials made available; radically different subjectivities projected. If the *FA* feels friendly to its habituated reader, then we must assume that *The Sun* feels at least equally friendly to its readers also. But these are very different kinds of friends: if you can tell someone's character by the friends they have, then we have here fundamentally different social subjects.

Class is clearly significant: and one difference between the *FA* and *The Sun* rests precisely on that. Some of you will know the German equivalent of *The Sun* in terms of the *Bildzeitung* type of readership: it looks very different; it makes available representational resources of a different kind, in a different manner. The front-page of the *Bildzeitung* offers (to the Anglo-Saxon type) a nearly chaotic welter of material: about 20 tiny "stories", 6 or 7 images, 5 or 6 advertisements, in no discernible order – to the English. If *The Sun* editor's assumptions about the subjectivities of his readership are correct, how can the *Bild* editor's assumptions about his/her audience also be correct? For one thing of course, there is precisely the question of habitus, as the product of a myriad of practices: *The Sun*, as the *Bild*, readers are habituated into adopting, transforming themselves into particular kinds of readers. The world has become one kind of world for the readers of *The Sun* and another for the readers of *Bild*. But beyond that I imagine that there looms the much larger question of culture. There is an affinity between the *FA* and the *Bildzeitung*, which mirrors an affinity between *The Guardian* and *The Sun*. The former offer plurality, heterogeneity: *Bild* to an extreme that becomes chaotic. The latter offer reduction, simplification: *The Sun*, to an extreme that becomes the stasis of total synthesis. My question is: how does one construct a multicultural, in this case a European subject, given this difference?

That is one question, relevant for educationists in England at the moment. A more general question is posed by the title of Freire's new book **The Pedagogy of Hope**. How can we, in our own areas bring about the aspirations of his newly formulated, and essential pedagogic and political project? For me, working in the area of representation and education, it lies in two directions. One is about the remaking of linguistic and semiotic theories in ways which acknowledge the agentive character of social subjects in their self-transformation, and, in this process, their production of the means of representation and new transformation. The other lies in a constant examination of my role as a teacher, who assists the learner in making available to him or to her some of the necessary resources for their transformation, in the larger context of a project of the liberation of human potential.

REFERENCES

Bourdieu, P. (Ed J. Thompson). *Language and symbolic power*. Cambridge: Polity Press, 1992.

Freire, P. *The Pedagogy of the Oppressed*. Harmondsworth: Penguin, 1972

Kress, G. R. . 'Against Arbitrariness: on the Social Production of the Sign as a foundational issue in Critical Discourse Analysis'. *Discourse and Society*, Volume 4, No 3, 1993.

Discussing Paulo Freire:

Literacy Among Surrey Sixth Formers

Jennifer Chew

About fifteen years ago, soon after I started my present job teaching English in a Surrey sixth form college, there was a ring at my doorbell one afternoon. Outside was a small boy of perhaps seven clutching an exercise-book. He looked at me rather suspiciously and said: 'Are you the spelling lady?' I was taken aback. The strange thing was that I had just started making noises about the spelling problems I was noticing among my students – but I did not think that this could have earned for me, even locally, the title of 'the spelling lady'.Fortunately, his father was still hovering in his car and we established that they had come to the wrong address, so the child was whisked off to some 'spelling lady' who was presumably rather more prepared for his arrival than I was. Since then, I think a number of people have come to think of me the 'spelling lady'. It is true that spelling has become a particular interest of mine, but I hope to convince you that I see literacy as extending far beyond spelling in particular and the 'basics' in general – although I think that the 'basics' are a pretty good place to start and a good basis on which to build, at least in conventional school education – and conventional school education, rather than the sort of thing we have heard about from Paulo Freire, is all that I can talk about from first-hand experience. My perception is that many 16-year-olds in England today are being prevented from attaining the higher levels of literacy that we would wish for them by the fact that the nuts and bolts of literacy are not securely in place.

When I realised what the line-up was today – that I would be the only female and non-professor on the platform during this session – I was sorely tempted to develop acute appendicitis. And then I though that perhaps you *ought* to hear from someone who has been an ordinary classroom English teacher since the 1960s and has enjoyed it enough to stay at the chalkface. I was comforted yesterday to realise that I met at least one of Paulo Freire's requirements for a good teacher – I love the students and the job enough to have stuck at it for most of the past thirty-two years. I qualified as a teacher in

South Africa in 1961, and taught in state secondary schools there for most of that decade. I then took an eight-year break in order to be at home with my children when they were young, and in 1978 I started my present job teaching Surrey sixth-formers. Three-quarters of my time is now taken up with teaching English at Advanced Level – separate language and literature courses, both of which I enjoy very much. The other quarter of my time is taken up with GCSE 'resit' English classes and with the special needs in the college. These last two have involved me in working closely with students who have problems with basic literacy, although clearly the phrase 'problems with basic literacy' means something rather different in Surrey from what it means in Brazil. My thesis, however, is that, in this country at least, underachievement in literacy relative to ability is probably almost universal, and that we need solutions which take this into account.

As I have said, at least three-quarters of my time is spent in teaching at levels where, if I insisted on doing nothing but the 'basics', it would soon show in disastrous exam results. In reading, A-Level students need to be able to cope with different genres and styles, and with irony, bias and other subtleties in texts; in writing, they need to handle language fluently, enthusiastically and appropriately for the purpose for which they are writing. The purposes to which my students put their literacy are, I feel, their own business – it may be to fight oppression, or to read Plato, as Paulo does, or to keep in touch with current events by reading newspapers intelligently, or to meet the requirements of the workplace. I don't see my task as preparing them for a particular use of literacy.

I find, however, that too many of my A-Level students struggle because they do not have a secure enough grasp of the mechanics of language to read and write at an appropriate level. Most are now functioning below their potential, in spite of the fact that they have GCSE results far above the national average. They *should* be reading widely and understanding what they read extremely well, but the fact is that they understand very little without help. Their mis-understandings often arise from the misreading of quite simple words: I have had a student taking the part of Malvolio in *Twelfth Night* and reading 'commended' as 'condemned' and 'surly' as 'surely'. Vocabulary tends to be very weak, even among A-Level English students: the word 'rebuked' cropped up in a half-term assessment exercise last week and several students did not know its meaning. This is not a purely local problem: a recent A-Level English Examiners' Report commented that candidates generally seemed to be functioning with a smaller vocabulary than in the past, which suggests that the phenomenon that we are noticing is quite widespread. Writing, even among those with high grades for GCSE English, is often pedestrian, inaccurate and difficult to understand. A second-year A-Level English Language student analysing a passage for the archaic features in vocabulary, grammar and syntax wrote the following largely unpunctuated piece last week:

> *"The aspects of vocabulary within the piece or a piece are many it is however most appropriated in this case to comment on the Archaic Useage and also the word meanings i.e. the fact that the meaning of a word may of changed over the years, therefore if each word that fits into this catorgory is taken and anaylised seperate to all the others this results would lead thus . . . "*

Six weeks ago, I asked my new A-Level English Literature students to write for twenty minutes in their first lesson with me about the reading they had done for GCSE and about their tastes in reading generally. One, with an A for GCSE Literature, produced the following:

> *"I didn't enjoy reading Macbeth as I found it difficult to understand, as I went along it got easier. We wrote about 3 soliloquys which once I understood were quite easy to write about. I enjoyed 'An inspector calls' as I found it interesting and the ending completly shocked me. I read a lot of Dick Francis books which I find very interesting, the books contain a lot of action and mystery which I enjoy. I liked the Virginia Andrews books although they become a bit repeatitive but some, especially 'flowers in the attic' were very good."*

Socio-economic factors are not the problem, at least in our area. We are in leafy Surrey, and virtually all our students have English as their first language. Many come from well-off homes: about half of those who are old enough to do so drive to college in their own cars – the numbers have increased so much over the past three or four years that the college has had to build a student car-park, which suggests increasing affluence rather than increasing poverty. The exam results with which the students arrive have always been markedly better than the national average and have improved in line with the national trend. At the same time, however, standards of spelling among our intake have declined. We have used the same spelling test for the past ten years as a mass screening device to identify students with literacy problems, and the average score on this test has dropped significantly over the years. At the bottom end of the ability-range, we have students who seem to have little conception of the logic of spelling. One of my students recently puzzled me by writing a word which could have been 'nearly' (except that the context made this unlikely) or 'rearly'.

It turned out that he meant 'really'. I asked him if he could spell 'real', and he could. I then pointed out that 'real' and 'really' were related, one being the adjective and one being the adverb. He knew no grammar, so the terms 'adjective' and 'adverb' meant nothing to him – but it would have helped if he had just been taught that knowing that there are relationships between words can help with spelling. I did not remember encountering problems like this when I taught in South Africa, but I don't like relying on subjective impressions so I took some trouble to run objective checks when I visited there in 1987 and 1992. I used the same test as I use with my Surrey students and tested the same age-group, though in ordinary state secondary schools rather than in the equivalent of a sixth form college. On each occasion, mixed-ability samples, of several hundred predominantly (but by no means exclusively) white English-speaking youngsters, there achieved a significantly higher average score on the test than my sixth-formers. A group of Zulu-speaking youngsters in a very poorly-resourced school achieved an average score only marginally below that of the Surrey students and the lowest score in the Zulu school was four times as high as the lowest from my Surrey students. I'd like to read a paragraph from an essay by a Zulu-speaking 16-year-old on black South African poetry after the 1976 Soweto riots. The girl had herself been brought up in Soweto:

> *"In form, 'City Johannesburg', a pre-1976 poem, paradoxically displays, through its relatively long lines, a kind of luxurious suffering – as if the victims of apartheid could forever lament and suffer with occasional feelings of bitterness. The fairly long lines symbolise the endless oppression and the misery the poet is always confronted with in Johannesburg. The long lines function effectively as conscience-stirring laments. The poem '1976', in contrast, consists of short, tense lines which seem to stress the futility of words and the loudness of deliberate silence."*

This girl's teacher might well be considered reactionary in this country – he told me that he believed passionately in teaching spelling and formal grammar. His methods seem to have worked extremely well: not only do his pupils make few errors with spelling and punctuation – the best of them also express themselves with an elegance and a fluency that I seldom get from my own students.

We *do* have problems in England, although they are very different from those in Brazil. I believe that we must address our own problems in ways which are appropriate to the local situation. My own diagnosis of what has happened is that as teachers have moved towards the view that the 'basics' are not *all-*

important, which is a view that I would share, many have moved rather too far in the direction of the view that the 'basics' are *not at all* important. I am not suggesting that there are teachers who would explicitly subscribe to the latter view, but that the movement along the spectrum has been in that direction and that some have moved too far. Students are telling us that teachers in their previous schools have not taught or corrected spelling and punctuation. I realise that the students' perceptions of these things are not always reliable, but some *do* manage to support their statements with samples of work. I believe that children who have been *taught* the mechanics of English in a structured way and in easily manageable steps are better off, in the long term, than those who are expected to infer a great deal for themselves. Spelling is something which, I believe, can be taught in ways which make it extremely interesting and which mesh in with other aspects of language-teaching – while learning about the principles of spelling, children can, for example, be taught about relationships between meaning and spelling, about etymology, about grammar and morphology. If teachers teach spelling well, they are teaching much more than spelling and are giving children an invaluable sense of the structure of language. My own view is that more explicit teaching about the mechanics of language, far from being reactionary, would make children much more powerful language-users than they are at the present.

Discussing Paulo Freire:

Empowerment for the Individual or the State?

Roy Carr-Hill

Paulo has given us a very stimulating presentation. I want to focus mainly on large scale literacy programmes in the South which was the focus of much of Paulo Freire's work. In particular, I shall address my remarks to three points he made: the Cultural Baggage of the literacy pursuit; the Political Baggage of a literacy programme; and the viability of Mass Campaigns. Whilst, in keeping with the celebratory mood, the treatment of the first two will be relatively light-hearted, I hope the seriousness of the points are appreciated.

CULTURAL BAGGAGE

Paulo's story of the student struck me: not that he (PF) gave 10/10 to a reactionary, but his willingness to tell us the maximum mark. When I was first in Mozambique in 1978-81, there were interminable discussions in faculty boards about students marks such as 8, 10, 12 or 14. Because of my very limited Portuguese at the time, it took me several meetings to pluck up the courage to ask what was the maximum mark. Once my language had been understood, it took about half an hour for my colleagues to realise what question I was asking: for it had been ordained in the Metropolis (Lisbon) - and accepted without question by FRELIMO, the vanguard party - that all marks were out of 20 (I still don't know why).

It was also in Mozambique that many of us 'cooperantes' - a strange phenomenon - found ourselves obliged to carry around a 'bureaucracy bag' because of the extensive range of requirements in any official application e.g. for a holiday, we needed to have so many fiscal stamps, for a visa another set of fiscal stamps, and all on blue paper with 25 lines. Every paper had to be ceremoniously stamped and one of the few thriving industries was the rubber stamp making business. Anarchic Anglo-saxons like ourselves took to using a stamp inscribed I AM A HUMAN BEING.

The phenomenon was clearly Lusophone: during my only visit to Brazil, I spent half a day transfixed in front of the Minister of De-Bureaucratisation which appeared in Brazil after the 'abertura'. Only in the Portuguese language, could one invent such a concept as a *Ministry* for De-Bureaucratisation.

The importance of understanding what literacy is, how it is perceived, and its relation to praxis and social development should not be underestimated. Having been forgotten for several years, the issue of literacy has once again become a 'priority' in the industrialised countries of the North, on the presumption that it is a prerequisite for continued economic domination of the South and international competitiveness (CERI, 1992). Major national institutions in several countries in the North (Bengtsson, personal communication) are launching large scale surveys of functional literacy - ignoring all the work that has been carried out in the South - in order to identify target groups for re-education. Yet among the many things we have learnt from Paulo, surely one thing stands out: people don't become literate through training but because they *decide* to. Literacy cannot be imposed on a pliant reserve army of labour; it forms part of the practice of liberation from slavery.

POLITICAL BAGGAGE

There are dangers in promoting politicisation as a vehicle of literacy. Whilst there is good evidence of the importance of national commitment and the political will to implement a large scale campaign (Carron and Bordia, 1985), and indeed, one can argue that the State has to be the prime mover for a successful mass campaign (Lind, 1988), there are possible pitfalls. The Mozambican campaign provides an example.

Thus in the National Literary Seminar held in 1975, it was advocated that the literacy tutor had to have a "sound political training" (Lind, 1988). The implications of this in terms of indoctrination and, a fortiori, undermining any democratic process were not discussed.

Similarly the key words were to be taken from statements which were clearly govenment self aggrandisement rather than concepts emerging from the praxis of the illiterates themselves. For example,

> *"FRELIMO as the vanguard party continues the struggle. Organised by FRELIMO, the people struggle against hunger, lack of clothing, Xiconhoca and the exploitation of man by man."*

All of us would be sympathetic with the intentions behind this statement. However, the extent to which the blatant paternalism was, in fact, an impediment to effective mobilisation is unknown.

A more recent example is related to the curious involvement of the World Bank in the literacy campaign in Ghana. The World Bank has, on the whole, kept out of literacy programmes as being 'too political' - and anyway not cost effective (Roman, 1990). But they have become involved in Ghana which is seen - at least temporarily - as the success story of structural adjustment in Africa.

The Ghanian campaign claims to draw on Freire as informing their pedagogy and implicitly uses Freirean ideas to justify the politicisation of their programme (that's not Paulo Freire's fault, of course).

In their 'pilot year', held just before the first general elections, the political education class, programmed into the schedule, included teaching how to vote. Learners were shown a ballot paper along the following lines (with names of Ghanian political parties changed to British 'equivalents' for purposes of comprehension).

Figure 1 - The Ballot Paper

LABOUR	
LIBERAL	
FASCIST	

After having been shown what a ballot paper looked like, learner participants were then shown how to vote, by putting a cross like this:

Figure 2 - How to Complete a Ballot Paper

LABOUR	
LIBERAL	
FASCIST	X

Given that this would have been the first time that most people had ever voted, and probably the first time that people in rural areas would have heard of the process of voting, the capture of a significant part of the rural vote by Flt. Lt. Rawlings' governing party was not, therefore, a great surprise.

SUCCESS OR FAILURE OF MASS CAMPAIGNS

There have been several approaches to promoting literacy, but the most emotive is the mass campaign. The theory is similar to that of the short sharp shock. Examples of successful campaigns include Cuba (1952), Nicaragua (1982), and Southern Vietnam (1986). These were characterised by:

- momentum of commitment (recent conquest of power);
- relatively low rate of illiteracy (Cuba 24%; Nicaragua 50%);
- one principal majority language;
- effective mobilisation (formal schools were closed to release teaching personnel).

In other countries, with much higher literacy rates (e.g. Angola, Burma, Ethiopia, Mozambique, and Tanzania), the repeated long march strategy was employed in the form of rolling (sometimes annual) literacy campaigns. These were and still are usually launched in the context of a general attack on underdevelopment.

These have tended to fail both because these situations are much more difficult (with low rates of literacy and a diversity of languages) but also because the political commitment expires.

For, without someone like Paulo Freire, or someone similarly motivated, the pedagogical methodology proposed is, whilst fervently discussed by academics, only adopted in a very emaciated form or even *institutionalised* in, for example, occupation-specific training schools.

Furthermore, it seems unlikely that a mass centrally directed campaign will ever work. This is for several reasons: a programme which is sensitive to local concerns, must rely on local knowledge; there are inter-district variations which make a programme, which is successful in one place, of doubtful applicability in another, and so on.

Moreover, I think that one has to question whether, in the developing country context, everyone is motivated to become literate. The evidence from two empirical studies in the South, in Kenya and Tanzania, is presented below (Table 1). Those who come to literacy campaigns are already motivated, often already partly schooled. Those who have not already experienced schooling tend not to come. A mass campaign attempting to reach the poorest of poor who have not been to school has an almost impossible task.

Table 1: Learners in Kenyan and Tanzanian Literacy Programmes: their previous attendance at Primary School

	Kenya	*Tanzania*	
	All Ages	*All ages*	*Those aged 45+*
	%	%	%
None	44	40	49
A little	36	13	14
4+ years	20	47	37

Carr-Hill and Carron (1994)

Paulo explained how he has asked to become national coordinator of a literacy campaign for Brazil in January 1964; but that the coup of April 1964 effectively put an end to any possibility of a mass campaign along the lines he had suggested. Given the preceding analysis of mass campaigns, whilst we are, of course, very lucky that to have Paulo with us, perhaps he was lucky he was not given the opportunity to fail.

REFERENCES

Carr-Hill, R.A. and Carron, G. "What Role is Literacy Playing" submitted to *Comparative Education Review,* 1994.

Carron, G. and Bordia, A. (Eds) *Issues in Planning and Implementing Literacy Programmes.* Paris: International Institute for Educational Planning, 1985.

Centre for Educational Research and Innovation *Adult Illiteracy and Economic Performance.* Paris: OECD/CERI, 1992.

Freire, P. *Pedagogy of the Oppressed.* Penguin: Harmondsworth,1972.

Lind, A. *Adult Literacy: Lessons and Promises.* Stockholm: Institute of International Education Studies in Comparative and International Education, No 12, 1988.

Roman, R. *Non Formal Education: an Evaluation of Programmes and Projects.* 1990.

Reply to Discussants

Paulo Freire

I am not sure whether I will succeed but I will try to give answers to the three questions raised here. I will start by replying to the first one which refers to newspapers in Brazil. Generally speaking, I think that we have not yet got a newspaper able to write in popular language. When I say popular language I am saying something about the syntax of the working class, and the semantics of the working class. I will not speak about pronunciation because this is not necessary. Generally we write for the people, the popular mass, in the same language as you demonstrated in the second and third page of *Folha de São Paulo*[1]. Usually, newspapers are elitist. Like the *Folha de São Paulo*, the *Estadão* tries to reach the popular areas, but only on the front page. The other pages are written for us, the educated people. There are also newspapers which think that they are trying to communicate with the popular sectors. But all they do is to report on crimes. That is for me a very mistaken view of what people understand. These papers reduce the ability of people to read and understand by focusing only on crimes, deaths, and accidents. Also, the language is terrible.

When we are working with literacy programmes (and there are groups in Brazil doing it very well), we have first to challenge the students to begin to write their own texts. It is impossible to split reading from writing, and from speaking. When we start speaking we have already inside us the ability to speak, and the possibility to write. This phenomenon is an historical one, from the earliest times: human beings started saying the words after they had transformed reality. Firstly they transformed reality; secondly they gave names to that transformation, to the objects. In the evolutionary process, the first human beings already had the possibility to write the words they were speaking. Today, when a child begins to grasp language socially (no one teaches language to anyone; we teach grammar, but not language which we grasp socially through social practice) she or he is just waiting for writing. One of the scandals of high levels of illiteracy is that illiteracy represents a violence against the natural possibilities and the natural tendency of human beings. This is a crime. To prevent people from writing and reading is a violence. It is a kind of castration of human beings.

In a way we are preventing human beings from doing something which they have the right to do i.e. to read and to write.

But, the process of reading does not mean literally reading written words. Above all comes reading the world as an anticipation of reading words. We first read reality and afterwards we read the texts. In other words, we first read the context and afterwards we read the text. Reading the text must be preceded by the reading of the context. In the last analysis reading texts is a dialectical exercise which leads us permanently to the reading of the original context. One of the mistakes we make as professors at the university is the mystification of reading written words. I know of some examples where graduate students are asked in one semester to read three hundred books. That explains how some suicides happen. I always ask myself if those professors have really read three hundred books. There is also the case of professors who suggest the reading of some books from page 5 to page 25. Why? What right do I have to say to the students that they are able to read just from page 5 to page 25? What I should say is that such a chapter has challenged me a lot. As a result I read these books. I can say that, but I cannot determine the pages for the students to read. This is an authoritarian stance by the teacher.

I now would like to come back to the problem of reading and writing. I am sure that cultures such as ours as well as African cultures are dominantly, and sometimes totally, based on oral language. The experience is an experience of an oral culture. The memory is oral, as in Africa. To work in cultures such as those is completely different from working in those cultures which have a strong experience of written language. I remember when I came to Paris in May 1968 at the very moment of the Sorbonne invasion. In June, I bought 25 essays which had been published about me. This is an example of a reading and writing culture. The French people write their history every day. I do not know if they write very well, but they do write. I then said to myself that in Brazil we only have two or three books about 1964. Even today we do not have solid books analysing for example some very important aspects of popular education before the 1964 coup d' état. It is very sad that a book in Brazil is considered a bestseller if three thousand copies are sold in the first edition. But three thousand copies should be sold just in a small neighbourhood of São Paulo. We have 14 million people in São Paulo. However we do not have one million readers. Much depends on the lack of spending money for books; also many people are not able to read; and, lastly, a good number do not like to read, even if they are at the university. One of the things we should do in Brazil is to increase and to improve the experience of reading.

You asked my opinion about the degree of elitism and of populism in different sections of the *Folha de São Paulo*. I think that maybe all the big newspapers in Brazil have this dual characteristic. Some newspapers are formally elitist. Others are completely elitist. I think that the **Estadão** is a totally elitist newspaper, nevertheless, it attempts to transfer elitism to the masses. Suppose I am an elitist man. I could well think of techniques to use in order to encourage the readers to be elitist like me. This is a political and ideological task. I think that completely elitist newspapers do that. The formally elitist newspapers are elitist from the tactical point of view. I think that this is not good. A progressive newspaper would have to reach the masses without having to make such a concession. I would have to study, I would have to do some research in order to reach the people with less difficulty. But not through a kind of concession like this. I should be consistent in my choices.

As regards the second question, I have to confess to all of you that when I think about language, when I try to understand the mysteries of the language, i.e. how language is acquired socially, I am especially concerned with the political dimension of the language. I have been trying to work as much as I can on a scientific approach and on scientific findings which could help me to minimize mistakes, but my real preoccupation has been a political one. Of course, ethically speaking, I think that in everything we have to consider the ethical, as well as the aesthetic aspects. I never separate one from the other, they come together. I think that ethical behaviour is beautiful. I have really been trying to make the process of teaching how to read and to write very political. It does not make sense, for example, to teach the Brazilians how to read and write through a method that does not stimulate ways towards possible changes in the reality of Brazil. It is as if I am saying to those illiterate people that what they need immediately is simply to write and read the words. But, to write and to read what? To write and to read in favour of what? That is, what is our objective in reading? Reading for me is not a neutral activity. I read because I need to read, because I need to transform the reality into something better. The good books are those which challenge me in understanding reality better and, consequently, I become more competent to transform that reality.

I am a politician 24 hours a day. This does not mean, nevertheless, that I am a candidate for the Senate of Brazil. I do not feel competent for that. But as an educator, my work is always illuminated by my political choice. Of course we cannot be politicians singlemindedly. We also have to have science. No matter which country and the culture we are working in, it is impossible to think about literacy without reading Piaget and Vygotsky. How can I understand the very process of acquiring language without reading Vygotsky? I am only sorry that I did not find Vygotsky until ten years ago. Prior to that time Vygotsky was unknown in Brazil and in Latin America. Similarly I only read Gramsci when I was in exile. I read Gramsci and I discovered that I had been greatly influenced by Gramsci long before I had read him. It is fantastic when we discover that we had been influenced by someone's thought without even being introduced to their intellectual production.

Of course we have to be very careful in our teaching, whether we are teaching literacy or any other discipline. We should always do it well. Those of us who have some experience in teaching literacy to adults recognize how difficult is the moment when a worker of forty, thirty, or twenty years of age holds a pen for the first time. It is a rather different experience when, for example, I naturally pick up a pen to write. My brain controls the strength I have to use, in order to manipulate the instrument. But the worker never had before this idea of the relationship between the strength the brain puts in the action and the weight of this instrument. His experience had been so far with an axe or a hammer. He then transfers the same command to the muscular system when holding the pen. The other difficulty they face is the lack of confidence. I remember, when I lived in Recife, I hired a painter, an illiterate worker, to paint the rooms of my house. In one of the rooms I had asked him to draw a horizontal line about ten to fifteen centimetres to the ceiling, as it was very fashionable at the time. The decorator came to the room and did the proper measurement in order to draw the horizontal line up to which he would have to paint. I was fascinated with the way he did it. He measured the wall and hammered two small nails one in each corner to get the same height. Then he linked both nails with a string which had a kind of brown colouring. He then went up a ladder, held the string with the tip of his fingers, pulled the string, releasing it immediately afterwards. And there was the line drawn on the wall. It was perfect. He did not shake at all when he did it. However, in the circle of culture every time he had to use a pencil, he could not hold it still; his hand used to shake.

In Brazil I used to start my literacy lessons with a discussion about culture. It was a very simple conversation with ten codifications, whose reading or decodification would give us an introductory understanding of what culture is about. I was full of happiness when I started to perceive the results of that discussion – when the illiterate workers realised that to make culture was also to transform a world which had not been made by them. They understood that culture also came from the processes of transformation of the world which we accomplish. Culture was also a poem, as if created by a great poet. It was the sculpture of a great artist. But it was also the way they spoke. In many occasions I heard the workers in the circles of culture saying things such as " I do this, therefore I make culture". Only then had the illiterates finally understood that we can transform a reality which we did not make, and we can transform the reality which we make. History, culture, politics – all these things are made by us. But, if I can transform the world which I did not make with or without a sophisticated technology, we are also able to transform reality, historically and politically. Thus they got much confidence in themselves through the simple discussion of culture. That is what culture really means. I firmly believe that it is much more important for the illiterate to understand their context, than just to be able to read in an alienated way. For me, the question of how to teach, to read, and to write is immediately linked to a political issue. This does not mean, for example, that in literacy classes for adults, you never have time to teach them how to read and to write because you are making politics. This is wrong. This is an absurdity. If we are there to teach them how to read and to write that is what we must do. But, in doing that, we can never dissociate the teaching of writing and reading from the understanding of reality. Further, from an ethical point of view, we do not have the right to say to the illiterate that the only good thing is to belong to the Workers' Party. No, I do not have this right. But, I have the duty to say that there are five, six, seven parties. I have the duty to discuss the ideology and the political choices of these different parties. I have also the duty of telling them which is my choice. I do not accept neutrality which is to have a kind of hypocritical posture in the world. What I cannot do is to lie, or to impose my choice upon them.

I now turn my attention to the third question raised by my discussants. This question is very interesting. I have been asked if, had the 1964 coup d' état in Brazil not happened, my work would have failed or succeeded. First, it is too difficult to answer a question like that in historical terms. But it is a good question. At least some Brazilians, in their negative criticism of my work, were able to find something positive by saying that one of my major pieces of luck was the coup d'état. In their view the coup spared me a tremendous disaster. I am not sure about that. On the contrary, I think that if the coup d' état had not happened we would have been very successful all over Brazil. We had examples of success. In Brasília, for example, for three or four months we had the opportunity to work with thousands of illiterate workers. We organized three hundred cultural circles, around Brasília in the satellite towns, with excellent results. The first experience in Northeast Brazil, in Angicos, in the State of Rio Grande do Norte[2], was also very good. I had there three hundred illiterate workers reading and writing just before the coup d' état. Recently my wife and myself went there. We met ten of those three hundred illiterate workers. One of them was an old man, eighty-five years old, but still in very good health. In the sixties he had made a fantastic speech to the President of Brazil, João Goulart when he visited Angicos. We also met a forty-two year old woman, the daughter of a couple of illiterate workers who had followed the programme. As a child she used to come with her parents to the circle. There she learned how to read and write. She told us that when President Goulart visited Angicos he was so impressed with her ability to read a newspaper that he promised her a gift. When asked what she would like to have, she said she wanted a school bag. She got it. More importantly, she became a teacher because of that experience. When asked by my wife what she would like to have now as another gift, she said: "Dignified treatment for teachers." What a fantastic demand! Of course, she did not learn that with the literacy process. She learned it through life, by living and by experiencing herself the lack of respect with which the politicians in Brazil and the State treat educators. It is a colonial tradition. Brazil in this aspect, and in some others, is still a colony.

Therefore I think I can say that, if it were not for the coup d'état, we would have had major success. Two main reasons permit me to say that. First, my work had been embedded in the theoretical foundations of psycholinguistics and sociolinguistics. These two fields of study are nowadays very much oriented by the writings of Vygotsky and Luria. I acknowledge also that most probably the recent contributions of sociolinguistics would perhaps make me review some of my previous experiences.

The second reason needs to be explained in the context of Brazil's political momentum. Brazil entered the fifties and sixties with a populist government. New power relations had been developed between the popular and the ruling classes. This populist political alliance is sometimes very interesting because it is ambiguous. The populist leader stimulates people to political participation and, simultaneously, sustains a political option to that of repression. This contradiction is well represented by the popular saying: to light a candle to God and another to the devil. The populist leader needs the support of the masses. Without the masses on the streets, for example, it would be impossible for the government to act along the lines of populism. Then what happens (and this is the main contradiction or ambiguity of the populist system)? The leader invites the people to the squares and to the streets because he or she needs the masses' participation. This becomes a practice. The masses learn how to come by themselves. In a given moment in the populist experience there are two options: one is to transform the populist experience into a revolutionary experience with the populist government being forced to commit suicide in order to be born again as a revolutionary one. This is very difficult. The other option is for the Right to seize power because of the political emptiness. In the sixties Brazil went through that experience with Goulart, a real populist leader, a greater leader than any among the right wing. Under Goulart there was mass participation in Brazilian political life. The masses could be seen in the streets; they could be heard using a different language.

I remember a very interesting event which illuminates well my point. Being Brazilian, I really enjoy football. My team in Recife was Santa Cruz, the team of the masses. All its supporters were fanatic to the point of crying and tearing up their membership cards every time Santa Cruz lost a game. Once I was at the stadium, in the part favoured by the masses. I noticed nearby a very well dressed man, in a white suit, and a tie, very unusual. He was probably a supporter of Náutico, the opposite and aristocratic team. He was most certainly out of place in that part of the stadium. Santa Cruz was winning by three goals to nil. Suddenly, a young black and healthy Santa Cruz supporter, full of emotion and enthusiasm, looked at the Náutico group of supporters and addressed them in a very dirty language: "What a bunch of assholes!" The smart man reacted by taking out his membership card and saying arrogantly: "I do not permit such a language in my presence". The black youngster, with no hesitation, stood up and replied, looking first at his friend and then at the arrogant man: "That chap is completely mad. Look, you had better put your card back in your pocket. Otherwise I will take it, tear it up, and beat you up". This was said in incorrect syntax, but full of rhythm. I enjoyed the dialogue very much and the prompt counter-reaction of the elegant man: he put his card back in his pocket and left. This would never have happened fifty years earlier. In the early sixties it was completely viable. The coup d'état destroyed all that. After 1964 the dominant-dominated relationship was once again enforced. The open and primitive patterns of oppression that followed the coup d'état reached all social strata. My liberating theory was no exception. Thank you.

NOTES

1. Editorial Note: Gunther Kress, in his discussion during the Seminar, used examples from the *folha de São Paulo*, among other papers.

2. Editorial Note: Calazans Fernandes and Antonia Terra published recently a detailed account of the Angicos' experience, considered "the first experience, in Brazil . . . introducing the concept of dialogical learning in the teacher-student relationship." For further information, see: Fernandes, C. & Terra, A. *40 horas de esperança – o método Paulo Freire: política e pedagogia na experiência de Angicos* [40 hours of hope – Paulo Freire's method: politics and pedagogy in the Angicos' experience]. São Paulo: Ática, 1994.

Some Issues: Neutrality, Respect for the Students, Epistemological Curiosity, and International Financial Aid [1]

Paulo Freire

1.   NEUTRALITY

I repeat now that there is no neutral education. Not only for me. For you also. For everyone. It is important to think about the ethical and political consequences of the impossibility of the educational practice being neutral. Non-neutrality does not depend only on you or on me; it comes from the nature of the process. I would say it is ontological. It belongs to the nature of education. You raised the issue when you asked the question earlier. You said that if there is no neutral education who then establishes the ends, the objectives, the dreams? It is a very good question. I have a strong empathy with this ethical question. For me, what the real democratic teacher has to do is, first, make clear to the students of the impossibility of neutral education.

Second, I am convinced that dreaming is part of my ontology. In my point of view, philosophically speaking, it is impossible for one to be a human being without dreams. Dream is not a figure of speech such as a noun or an adverb or even an adjective in my existence. Human existence substantively demands dreams. There are lots of explanations for that, but I do not wish to use too much time in this issue. In spite of their individual nature, dreams are also historical and social. We produce dreams and we are produced by dreams in history. Then, the teacher would, as much as possible, make clear to the students that human existence implies the production of dreams which end up by producing human existence, and in this human existence, the conflicts, the choices, and the decisions – all these things are enveloped in and are enveloping my human and social existence.

Third, a good teacher who has a very solid and ethical posture has to proclaim to the students that she or he also dreams and what her or his dreams are about. I do not accept this kind of "neutered" teacher who hides her or his dreams because she or he is afraid of not respecting the students. No, I do not disrespect the students if I tell them the kinds of dream I dream: my utopia. I would disrespect the students if I try to impose on them, surreptitiously or clearly, my dream. Suppose, for example, that if you do not think like me, then I will not give you the grade you need to pass. This would be immoral. The teacher may well speak about her or his dream explaining that there are other dreams different from hers or his. But as a teacher I have the duty to fight in order to defend my dream. That is my presence in the world and means for me a permanent struggle in order to materialize my dream. My dream is not just to read books about the issues I love. I need to study, I need to read, and I need to become more and more competent. This is also my duty. It does not matter if I am reactionary or if I am progressive. What is important for the students is to know what is the choice. I think that one of the most important things for a teacher is to make her or his choice clear. It is equally important to make clear the duty and right she or he has to fight for this choice. The problem the teacher faces is how to be really careful not to impose her or his choice on the students who, in turn, must be the subjects of their own choice. I should make clear what my political choice is. I should also make clear to the students that I will try to convince them about my choice. Because of that I think that teaching is also an act of conversion. How is it possible for me to believe in some ideas and not to try to convince people that I am right? I could not teach.

The issue in teaching is not only to say that education cannot be neutral. This is a statement which I can prove scientifically, philosophically, epistemologically. But, this is not fundamental. For me this is only a starting point. What is fundamental for me is to defend my democratic position, and not only the right I have to eat well. I have to have indignation because in my country, Brazil, there are 32 million people in extreme poverty. I cannot sleep well if I do not say at least once a day that it is immoral. This is absolutely immoral. This is real pornography.

2.   ON HOW TO RESPECT THE CONTEXT OF THE STUDENTS AND TO BE EFFICIENT

This morning when I spoke about the qualities of the progressive teacher, I thought it was implicit in my speech that those qualities are not received as a gift nor do they exist outside of history, outside of context. The context of the school has to do with the context of the region, has to do with the context of the country, has to do with the context of the continent. What I want to say is that there is no history just inside the minds of the human beings. History is something concrete which make us while we are making it. I also spoke about the concepts of the democratic relationship between the teacher and the students.

I will tell you now a very interesting story. I personally lived at Harvard University and also at the University of Geneva. I remember Harvard, in 1969 (and it is not much more different today), I wrote two texts. In one I tried to make clear to the students what the act of reading and the act of studying meant for me. I remember being very careful – I did not want to give to the students as readers the impression that I did not believe in them as readers. I also gave some suggestions about reading: how to read a text, how to use the instruments without which we cannot read very well[2]. I wrote this paper and I wrote another one which I named 'draft programme' in which I said that the draft programme was to be discussed by all of us. Through our discussion we could then organize, create, and produce a new programme of activities. The programme belonged to us and not only to me. I have the right to make the programme and traditionally the teacher is the only one able to do that. But this is not fully true. We teachers have to work with the students. Then, in our first session I spoke to the students about my experience in Northeast Brazil, about my exile which was just beginning, about my reactions, and the cultural differences I was experiencing in the States, and those I had experienced in Chile. The following day we all agreed to discuss the draft programme and the paper on reading. I used to smoke a lot at that time. I smoked maybe three cigarettes in silence, absolute silence, the students over there and myself here, I am very patient and I kept on smoking and smoking. We were even able to hear the silence. How very uncomfortable it is when you can hear the silence! Then one of the students said: "Dr. Freire, I think I speak on behalf of my colleagues." The colleagues became very happy to having someone as a spokesman. He went on saying: "We found your text about reading very good. We think your draft programme should be the adopted programme."

Do you know what I did? This is the reaction of those who would like to continue to obey without struggling, without thinking, without discussing, without participating. There were two possibilities to make a tremendous mistake – politically, philosophically, and pedagogically speaking. The first possible mistake would have been to tell to the students that they were incapable, and lazy people, and that I was not going to work with them. The second possible mistake would have been to accept happily their conclusion and go home full of pride because the students of Harvard considered my draft programme an excellent programme. However I could not accept that. I told them that we were going to start discussing the first issue suggested on the programme immediately. I would speak for ten minutes. Afterwards, they would discuss what I had said. I started my short talk by challenging the students. Two months later we had finished the programme, working with questions and through challenges. I remember well that first day in Harvard. When I asked one of the students why he was asking me a question and what he was thinking of understanding in having asking this question, he did not know the answer. He did not know why he was asking the question. He did not know what he would like to know by asking the question. I explained that I could only ask a question if I knew the kind of knowledge I was lacking, and what I needed to become knowledgeable about the topic. That is the only reason for asking a question.

That experience with the students in Harvard was very interesting for me. I learned at that time that asking questions is a kind of pact between teachers and students. The students ask questions and teachers go home very happy because they can say that the students are alive in class. For me this is not enough. I do not want to know that the students are alive. I want to know that they are alive because they want to know something. I remember a similar situation in Geneva where I learnt a great deal from one of the students. We had a session to evaluate what we had done during the semester. One student said very bluntly: "Paulo, you made a mistake in the first seminar. You did not wait for us to "kill" you as a centralizer of power. You committed suicide in our presence. We were hoping to accept in time your 'death' as an authoritarian teacher. You should have remained alive so we could have 'killed' you.

This rather interesting observation shows us the need to act according to the situation of the students, the atmosphere of the country, the educational background of the students at home, and the tradition of the country. As teachers, sometimes we need to start a course by demonstrating our power. However, when during the course the power relations are re-balanced, we should never deny our authority. We should start by giving examples of what it means to be a democratic authority in the classroom, what it means to be an authoritarian authority. We must in many ways respect the context of the students in order to be efficient, and to help in the realization of our dreams. By doing so we are also able to demonstrate the impossibility of being neutral.

3. *EPISTEMOLOGICAL CURIOSITY*

As human beings, we should be absolutely aware that we have to face antagonisms. History is this. I remember in the seventies, some months after the publication of **Pedagogy of the Oppressed**, I received a letter from a young man from an Asian country. The letter read something like this: "Paulo Freire, I got the English translation of your book which I found very exciting. I invited a group of colleagues who are secondary school teachers to study your book. Immediately we started using your ideas. Soon afterwards we lost our jobs." I wrote back to him and I said that I had lost my job before having written the book. Therefore there is no neutrality in the world, and not only in education. I always say I cannot be neutral even when I say: Good morning! It depends on my intonation, and on my body movements. As teachers, we are inviting and challenging the students to be real human beings.

What is really to be a human being? Of course, there are lots of signs which tell us what a human being is about. When intellectually we ask ourselves which is the major characteristic that permits us to understand that we are human beings, we are then talking about epistemological curiosity. What is then epistemological curiosity? First I would like to point out that epistemological curiosity is an invention of human beings. As human beings, like any other animal, we are curious by nature. We are permanently aware of something around us. We are always in a state of constant desire to know about even the smallest things surrounding us i.e. a sudden noise. We turn around to understand what is happening. This is a simple and naive curiosity. But, when I speak about epistemological curiosity I am not referring to our natural pre-disposition towards the unknown. Epistemological curiosity is another kind of curiosity which is precisely that curiosity in which we have methodically organized spontaneous curiosity. What I want to say is that from that spontaneous curiosity I am able to build up another kind of curiosity which has a certain level of methodological rigour. Therefore I make it possible for the naive curiosity to become a serious and rigorous curiosity which methodically goes towards the object I have vis-à-vis myself and which I want to know. This epistemological curiosity explains the existence of science. The other (naive) curiosity stays at the level of common sense.

I am not saying here that we should be against common sense. On the contrary, we should respect it, and by respecting it, start from it to reach another degree of knowledge. This is what science does. Scientific discoveries are sometimes a result of mistakes. One of our tasks should be to de-mystify science. Positivism greatly emphasized one of the mistakes of science i.e. the belief in being certain. One of the characteristics of the postmodernism is not to be too certain. This is epistemological curiosity. It is through this kind of curiosity that we can approach the world, and ourselves. We ourselves are objects of our knowledge, and of our act of knowing. This also makes me a human being.

Suppose you are teaching economics. If you do not consider your students as human beings capable of using epistemological curiosity, there is no sense in your teaching. What you are doing is merely providing superimpositions of knowledge. What you have to do as a teacher is not to impose on the passive body of the student your package of knowledge. On the contrary, what you have to do is to challenge the epistemological curiosity of the student. This is to challenge, first of all, the body of the student in order for the body to organize her or his own epistemological curiosity. We are doing the opposite at the universities. We are covering the epistemological curiosity with a veil instead of unveiling knowledge. We do not improve epistemological curiosity. Even when reading books what we try to do is to memorize them and not to know the context of the book. The content of books can only become knowledge through epistemological curiosity. Nevertheless, to the extent that we begin to ask questions to provoke the epistemological curiosity of the students, without which it is not possible to know, their curiosity becomes more curious. The more curiosity is curious the more the rigidity of power is threatened. This is why under some political regimes we cannot ask questions precisely because to ask questions is to challenge.

I remember when I arrived in Geneva in the seventies and participated in a meeting with Christian ladies. A fantastic story was told. They said they where working in Geneva with immigrant children of Portuguese, Italian, and Spanish workers. They were teaching sexuality to those adolescent immigrants. One of the women said in her speech that the group was trying to get some financial help for the programme. They went to see some industrialists to whom they spoke about the experience. One of them agreed to give a large quantity of Swiss francs. Two months later this man received the ladies to report back on the programme. One of the ladies spoke very happily because she was totally convinced about the good results of the project. She pointed out how the teenagers were asking questions about sexuality, with no fear or inhibition. At the end, the industrialist said that he was immediately withdrawing any further help. The ladies were astonished. The industrialist went on to explain the reason for his decision: "If today, in the discussions about sexuality with these adolescents, they feel so free to ask questions, I wonder what kinds of question they will be asking when the issue is on social justice. I want workers who are well behaved, who are docile, and who do not ask questions". This is a good example of domination, of power.

Finally, because this issue is of an ethical nature, I wonder if we have the right to work against us. When we lose our job it is as if we are fighting against us. But it also depends on the understanding we have of what it means to work in favour of us. In my opinion, losing my job does not always means that I am working against me. Working against me always means to work against others. I would rather die. I prefer not to live if I say, for example, that it is decent and beautiful that 32 million Brazilians are prevented from eating. This is neither beautiful nor decent. It is immoral. It is an absurdity. It is a crime. What we have to do is to invite the students not to be silent vis-à-vis this immorality.

I defend in Brazil a kind of pedagogy I call 'pedagogy of the indignation'. This is the only way that can explain my presence in the world. It does not mean however that I am crazy. I have to have tactics to get and keep a job. It is necessary that the teacher knows, for example, to remain silent on Monday, and to speak out on the following Monday. We teachers must know also the context in which we are working to be able to perform the great job we have. The great job is to be in the world in order to do something positively for the transformation of the world.

4. INTERNATIONAL FINANCIAL AID

When I was Secretary of Education of the City of São Paulo, I was asked to receive a mission from the World Bank/Washington. In the meeting, to which I had also invited my assistants, the President of the mission said the purpose of their visit was to offer 50 million dollars to be spent in our programmes. I was puzzled because I had not asked for any loan. The offer was tied to some conditions. For example: I could use the 50 million dollars only in kindergarten schools. Secondly, the teachers should not necessarily have pedagogical training (he spoke about 'democracy' in the teaching process). I would have to give the 50 million dollars to private institutions which would not be responsible for paying back the loan. I would have to. There were other requirements but I discussed only these three. I then asked them one question: "Let us forget now the Bank and the Secretary of Education of São Paulo. Let us think of ourselves. Suppose that you ask me for three thousand dollars. I have just that to lend to you. But I will do that with some conditions. For example, I give you three thousand dollars but you have to buy fifty bits of underwear made in Recife; one hundred fifty pairs of shoes produced in Timbaúba (a town in Pernambuco, famous for its shoes); and ties made in São Paulo. Would you accept that?" They said they would not. I then said: "What makes you think that I would accept your offer? Who do think I am? A Brazilian who becomes Secretary of Education to betray his people? No. It would be better if our discussion finishes here. It is not possible for us to receive your money. I do not need your money. There is another reason why I say no to you. I will not help Brazil to increase its debt. I know what it means in monthly interest to pay back a large loan." I was asked another question which I thought was offensive: "If the Mayor, Luiza Erundina (a fantastic woman), accepts our offer, what would then happen?" I replied: "I will resign as Secretary and I will denounce her to the press. This is how I am, and I have nothing to do with your dreams." When I was asked about my conditions for accepting the money, my answer was: "You give us 50,000,000 dollars, and never ask anything about it. I will do what I think best with the money. The people of São Paulo will see the results of how the money is spent. I can never agree to paying it back to you. Thank you." The following day I went to the office of Mayor Erundina and I told her all about the meeting. Smiling, she said she had appointed me Secretary of Education because she was sure of my attitudes in situations like that one.

I do not want to give the impression to all of you that I am a sectarian person. No, I am not. I have written a lot of pages against sectarianism. I am radical. Yes, I am a radical man. I go deep. I think we have to talk with different people, including our opponents. I am always open to discussion. But, if we need money to implement educational projects and programmes, we must be the owners of the destiny of the money. No country or international agencies can ever impose conditions on anyone, on any country.

NOTES

1. These issues were raised by the audience in different moments of the Seminar.

2. For some scholars, consulting dictionaries or encyclopedias is a waste of time. For me, the use of these instruments is part of my reading and writing. I write for example three or four hours each day in my house and I consult dictionaries, encyclopedias, dictionaries of philosophy, of sociology, and of ideas. Sometimes I spend one in every four hours a day consulting dictionaries. I look for the meaning of words, for synonyms and antonyms. It is my work, my job and I cannot read without this exercise.

Afterword

Robert Cowen

As a student I met Socrates, though only in sculpture and writing and in pictures. I found that I admired him a lot, perhaps because I had spent most of my life talking like Glaucon. And if you talk like Glaucon any help you can get is much appreciated.

As a university teacher in the USA I met Freire, in writing, and later in person at the Institute of Education. I found that I admired him a lot, perhaps because I was talking, by then, like Socrates. And if you always talk like Socrates then any help you can get is much appreciated.

Both Socrates and Freire raise very disturbing questions, Socrates not least by the manner of his death, Freire by the facts of his life. How is it possible that such manifestly honest and gentle men may rouse the wrath of the State? Is it that States are dishonest and cruel? Everywhere and always? Macchiavelli thought so; or at least was precise in his specification of the virtue of princes. This is different from the virtue of ordinary men precisely because it demands dishonesty always and cruelty often. But this was long ago and far away: Athens, and Florence and Brazil, and has little to do with us, now and here. Or does it?

Britain is part of Europe and in the lifetime of the Institute, as measured in the personal lifetimes of its Directors, we have seen cruel and malevolent States persecute teachers unto death, sometimes in the name of ethnicity or race, sometimes in the cause of political correctness, and sometimes in the name of religion. At such extremes, the question for the teacher is probably not should you oppose the State, but, have you the courage and personal resources to do so? I have no clarity about my own reply, in practice and under specific conditions, in Nazi Germany or communist Poland, in Franco's Spain or in contemporary "Yugoslavia".

But neither Freire nor Socrates asked this question; though they both answered it. The question they did ask – what is it to be human in society and with which vocabularies and in which ways may we think aloud about that in public – produced a powerful pedagogy.

Note that this is not the more routine question of the intersection of the duties and rights of a citizen with the duties and rights of an organised profession of teachers in a dispute with Ministers of Education and politicians over how children should be educated; though the question can be extended to include this problem which clearly exercises many teachers in England now.

The indirect question posed by Socrates and Freire is a much older one and a more permanent one: at what point and on what terms may you stop your teaching? On what terms, if at all, do you permit yourself to stop your teaching if it is based on questions and **tentative** answers which your discussant (the "student") is free to renegotiate, by thinking, by checking facts, by arguing a position in public, by reading and by invoking daily experience or other peoples' books? No doubt the honourable and comfortable answer is, never. And no doubt the comfortable answer is that we have institutions with special rules and privileges – universities – precisely devoted to these values. Quite so; or almost quite so; or perhaps it was quite so. And anyway university teachers are such a vociferous lot that we can probably look after ourselves.

But do we routinely discuss with our students the highest, deepest and noblest responsibilities of the teacher, of the act of pedagogy, philosophically, sociologically, comparatively? Do we ever tackle the topic directly? Not now, I think, in a climate of competence, efficiency and skills. We used to. There was a magnificent course at the Institute when I was a student here on the Academic Diploma, in which we all read Plato and Aquinas and Rousseau, and Durkheim and Weber and Piaget and Mead and Bruner. We should probably re-inspect that idea, especially in a climate of competence and efficiency and skills. And if we do re-inspect that idea then I think much will be owed to Freire who in his writing over the years and in this book itself has reminded us freshly of some permanent questions which face all educators everywhere. His own answers are not only new, and put initially in the new context of Brazil. They are also disturbing answers, which we may wish to let disturb us.

APPENDIX

Excerpts from Paulo Freire's Curriculum Vitae

1. PUBLISHED BOOKS
(AS PROVIDED BY PAULO FREIRE)

1.1. Sole Author:

Education, the practice of freedom. London: Writers and Readers Publishing Cooperative, 1976. (First published in the United Kingdom under the title: *Education for critical consciousness.* London: Sheed & Ward, 1974)

Pedagogy of the oppressed. London: Sheed & Ward, 1972.

Extensão ou comunicação? [Extra-mural activities or communication?]. Rio de Janeiro: Paz e Terra, 1971.

Cultural action for freedom. Cambridge, Mass.: Harvard Educational Review, 1970.

Educação e mudança [Education and change]. Rio de Janeiro: Paz e Terra, 1979.

Pedagogy in process: the letters to Guinea-Bissau. London: Writers and Readers Publishing Cooperative, 1978.

Conscientização: teoria e prática da libertação [Conscientization: liberation theory and practice]. 3 ed. São Paulo: Moraes, 1980.

The politics of education: culture, power and liberation. South Hadley, Mass.: Bergin & Garvey, 1985.

A importância do ato de ler [The importance of reading]. São Paulo: Cortez, 1981. Coleção Polêmicas do Nosso Tempo, v.4.

Pedagogy of the city. New York: Continuum, 1993.

Pedagogy of hope. New York: Continuum, 1994.

Professora sim, tia não – cartas a quem ousa ensinar [Teacher yes, auntie no]. 2 ed. São Paulo: Olho d'água, 1993.

Política e educação: ensaios [Politics and education: essays]. São Paulo: Cortez, 1993. Coleção Questões da Nossa Época, v.23.

Cartas a Cristina [Letters to Cristina]. São Paulo: Paz e Terra, 1994.

1.2. Joint Publications:

Freire, P. et al. *Vivendo e aprendendo: experiências do IDAC em educação popular [Living and learning: IDAC experiences in popular education].* São Paulo: Brasiliense, 1980.

Freire, P. et al. *Paulo Freire ao vivo* [Paulo Freire live] São Paulo: Loyola, 1983.

Freire, P. & Illich, I. *Paulo Freire-Iván Illich: diálogo* [Paulo Freire-Iván Illich: dialogue]. Buenos Aires: Ediciones Búsqueda, 1975.

Freire, P. & Faundez, A. *Learning to question: a pedagogy of liberation.* New York: Continuum, 1989.

Freire, P. & Frei Beto. *Essa escola chamada vida [That school called life].* 7ed. São Paulo: Ática, 1991.

Freire, P. & Shor, Ira. *A pedagogy for liberation: dialogues on transforming education.* London: Macmillan, 1987.

Freire, P. & Guimarães, S. *Sobre a educação* (Diálogos) [About education (Dialogues)]. Rio de Janeiro: Paz e Terra, Volume I and II, 1982/1984.

Freire, P.; Gadotti, M. & Guimarães, S. *Pedagogia: diálogo e conflito* [Pedagogy: dialogue and conflict] 2ed. São Paulo: Cortez, 1986.

Freire, P. & Nogueira, A. *Teoria e prática em educação popular. Que fazer?* [Theory and practice in popular education. What to do?]. Petrópolis: Vozes, 1989.

Freire, P. & Guimarães, S. *Aprendendo com a própria história* [Learning from one's own history]. Rio de Janeiro: Paz e Terra, 1990.

Freire, P. & Macedo, Donaldo. *Literacy: reading the word and the world.* London: Routledge & Kegan Paul, 1987.

Freire, P. *Educación popular: un encuentro con Paulo Freire [Popular education: a meeting with Paulo Freire]*. Buenos Aires: Centro Editor de América Latina, 1988. Ed. Rosa María Torres (interviews).

Horton, M. & Freire, P. *We make the road by walking: conversations on education and social change*. Philadelphia: Temple University, 1990.

2. AWARDS

1975 – "Mahammad Reza Pahlevi" Award, Iran.

1979 – "Ordem do Mérito da Marim dos Caetés" Award – Olinda, PE, Brazil.

1980 – "King Baudouin" Award, Belgium.

1985 – "William Rayney Harper" Award from The Religious Education Association of United States and Canada – California, USA.

   – "Estácio de Sá" from the Rio de Janeiro Government, RJ, Brazil.

1986 – UNESCO Award for Education and Peace, Paris, France.

1987 – "Ordem Nacional do Mérito Educativo" from the Ministry of Education and Culture, Brazil.

1988 – "Frei Tito de Alencar" from the Mayor of Fortaleza, CE, Brazil.

   – "Mestre da Paz" from the Association of Research and Specialisation about Iberoamericans, Spain.

   – Medal of Merit of the City of Recife, Gold Class, Recife, PE, Brazil.

1990 – "Manchete de Educação", Brazil.

1990 – "International Merit" from the International Reading Association, Stockolm, Sweden.

   – Award from World University Service (SUM), São Paulo, Brazil.

1991 – Educator of the Year Award, Camara Municipal de Vereadores de Mogi das Cruzes, São Paulo, Brazil.

1992 – "Andres Bello" Award from the American States Organization (OEA), as The Latin American Educator, Washington DC, USA.

1993 – "Libertador da Humanidade" Medal from the Assembléia Legislativa da Bahia.

"DOCTOR HONORIS CAUSA"

1973 – Open University, Milton Keynes, England.

1975 – Catholic University of Louvain, Louvain, Belgium.

1978 – Michigan University, Ann Arbor, USA.

1979 – University of Geneva, Geneva, Switzerland.

1984 – Federal University of Pernambuco, Recife, Brazil.

1986 – New Hampshire College, New Hampshire, USA.

      – University of San Simon, Cochabamba, Bolivia.

1987 – University of Santa Maria, Santa Maria, Brazil.

1988 – University of Barcelona, Barcelona, Spain.

      – State University of Campinas, Campinas, Brazil.

      – Catholic University of Campinas, Campinas, Brazil.

      – Federal University of Goiás, Goiânia, Brazil.

      – Catholic University of São Paulo, São Paulo, Brazil.

1989 – University of Bologna, Bologna, Italy.

      – University of Claremont, Claremont, USA.

      – Institute Piaget, Lisbon, Portugal.

1990 – University of Massachussets, Amherst, USA.

1991 – Federal University of Pará, Belém, Brazil.

      – Complutense University of Madrid, Madrid, Spain.

1992 – University of Mons-Hainaut, Mons, Belgium.

      – Wheelock College, Boston, USA.

      – University of El Salvador, El Salvador, San Salvador.

1993 – Fielding Institute, Santa Barbara, USA.

      – Federal University of Rio de Janeiro, Rio de Janeiro, Brazil.

      – University of Illinois, Chicago, USA.

1994 – Federal University of Rio Grande do Sul, Porto Alegre, Brazil.

3. INSTITUTIONS AND CENTRES OF STUDY ON PAULO FREIRE

CEDIF – Centro de Estudos, Documentos e Informação Paulo Freire [Centre of Studies, Documentation and Information on Paulo Freire], São Paulo, SP, Brazil.

A.G. SPAK, Munich, Germany.

CAAP – Centro di Animazioni per L'Autogestione Popolare [Centre for Popular Self-Management], Alia, Italy.

CEDI – Centro Ecumênico de Documentação e Informação [Ecumenical Centre of Documentation and Information], São Paulo and Rio de Janeiro, Brazil.

CEG – Federal University of Espírito Santo, Vitória, ES, Brazil.

Center for the Study of Development and Social Change, Cambridge, Mass., USA.

Centro Vereda de Educação Popular [Vereda Centre of Popular Education], São Paulo, SP, Brazil.

Centro Pastoral Vergueiro [Vergueiro Pastoral Centre], São Paulo, SP, Brazil.

CIDOC – Centro Intercultural para Documentación [Intercultural Centre for Documentation], Cuernavaca, Mexico.

CEAAL – Consejo de Educación de Adultos para la América Latina [Council of Adult Education for Latin America], Chile.

INODEP – Institut Ecuménique au Service du Développement des Peuples [Ecumenical Institute for People's Development], Paris, France.

Institute of Adult Education, American Research Unit of Dar-Es-Salam, Tanzania.

LARU – Latin America Research Unit, Toronto, Canada.

MABIC – Mouvement d'Animation de Base International Outmeetings [International Movement of Popular Activities], Hasselt, Belgium.

Birgit Wingerrath, Due-Benst, Germany.

Research Library, Washington DC, USA.

SPE – Scuola Profissionale Emigranti [Vocational School for Immigrants], Zurich, Switzerland.

Syracuse University, Syracuse, USA.

OISE – The Ontario Institute for Studies in Education, Ontario, Canada.

The Paulo Freire Resauras Collection, Toronto, Canada.

UNIMEP – Methodist University of Piracicaba, Piracicaba, SP, Brazil.

UNISINOS – University of Vale do Rio dos Sinos, São Leopoldo, RS, Brazil.

University of Michigan, Ann Arbor, Michigan, USA.

Instituto Paulo Freire/São Paulo
c/o Prof. Moacir Gadotti
Rua Pedro Soares de Almeida, 114
05029-030 São Paulo – SP
Brazil
Fax: 55.11.873.04.62

Institute Paulo Freire/Los Angeles
c/o Prof. Carlos Alberto Torres
Graduate School of Education
UCLA
405 Hilgard Avenue
Los Angeles, California
90024-1521, USA
Fax:1.310.206.62.93

Contributors

Ana Maria de Araújo Freire, Researcher on the History of Brazilian Education. Former Senior Lecturer of History of Brazilian Education at the Catholic University of São Paulo (PUC/SP).

Denise Gastaldo, Currently a research student at the Institute of Education University of London supported by CNPq/Brazil.

Gunther Kress, Professor in the English, Media and Drama Department, Institute of Education University of London.

Jennifer Chew, English Tutor in Strode's College, Egham, Surrey.

Maria de Figueiredo-Cowen, Brazilian Lektor, Institute of Education University of London, and Brazilian Embassy.

Robert Cowen, Senior Lecturer in the Department of International and Comparative Education, Institute of Education University of London.

Roy Carr-Hill, Professor in the Department of International and Comparative Education, Institute of Education University of London.